The Art of
the Steal

Exposing Fraud &
Vulnerabilities in America's
Elections

Adrian Norman

Eleven Press

Copyright © 2020 by Adrian Norman.

Published by Eleven Press.

All rights reserved. No part of this publication may be reproduced, distributed or transmitted in any form or by any means, including photocopying, recording, or other electronic or mechanical methods, without the prior written permission of the publisher.

The Art of the Steal/ Adrian Norman. —1st ed.

Book Cover Design by JetLaunch.net

ISBN 978-1-64184-253-2 (pbk)

ISBN 978-1-64184-254-9 (eBook)

Contents

Introduction 5

01: Illegals Really Are Voting...11

02: Anomalies & Fraud In 2018 Midterm Elections 43

03: Dead Voters & Ghost Voters..81

04: Purging Voter Rolls 95

05: Ballot Harvesting 111

06: Voter I.D. & Voter Suppression 137

07: Presidential Advisory Commission On Election
Integrity...171

08: Google: Big Tech Leviathan Election Meddling.......183

09: Electronic Voting Systems 203

10 "Russian Collusion" and The Investigation Of Special
Counsel Robert Mueller...221

11: What Does Election Fraud Have In Common With
Alcoholism? 223

End Notes 241

About The Author...269

Introduction

After the election of President Donald J. Trump, questions swirled about the legitimacy of his presidency due to allegations that his campaign may have colluded with the Russian government in an effort to secure his victory. Those allegations ultimately led to the appointment of a special counsel to investigate and determine whether there was any truth to claims of "Russian collusion." Special Counsel Robert Mueller submitted his report to United States Attorney General William Barr on Friday, March 22, 2019. After a two-year investigation that cost taxpayers more than $30 million, not one U.S. citizen was charged with any crime related to conspiracy or collusion.

Many Americans voiced strong opinions over this investigation because this issue strikes at the core of our republic—the integrity of our elections and the ability of the people of this country to freely choose our own leadership through a fair, transparent process. It is "we the people" who bear the weighty responsibility of electing our own leaders. Outside interference in this process runs counter to the values of this nation and should not be tolerated.

The underlying issue with the "collusion" narrative was whether or not the American people were somehow defrauded in the 2016 election. And, although this case is now arguably the most talked about instance of suspected election fraud, presidential elections are not the only elections in which concerns about fraud are raised.

In 2018, Americans went to the polls and cast votes in midterm elections; many congressional seats were up for grabs. Days and weeks after the polls closed, there were lingering questions about the outcome of those elections after allegations of anomalies, irregularities, voter suppression and outright voter fraud in many states across the country, including the high-profile races in Georgia, Florida and Arizona.

In Georgia, Republican Brian Kemp ran against Democrat Stacey Abrams in a contentious race for governor. Two days before the election, Kemp opened an investigation after the state voter registration system was hacked. The cyber-attack was blamed on Democrats. Yet, allegations of racism were thrown back at Kemp, suggesting that he had voter rolls purged to influence the outcome of the election. Predictably, Democrats accused Republicans of voter suppression, and as many as four days after her election loss, Abrams refused to concede.

In Florida, heading into the weekend after the 2018 midterm election, federal officials descended upon Broward County after tens of thousands of "missing" ballots magically surfaced. This discovery immediately spurred allegations of fraud committed by the state's election supervisor, Brenda Snipes, who has been previously convicted for illegally destroying ballots as well as posting results of the 2016 election before the polls in her county even closed. Critics said that her checkered past of verified election meddling should have disqualified her from handling the 2018 election. They were also concerned that the anomalies taking place 2018 were yet another iteration of illegal activity, a brazen attempt to skew the results of an election in favor of candidates of her choosing.

In Arizona, GOP congressional candidate Martha McSally seemed to have narrowly won a heated battle against Democrat Kyrsten Sinema. Shortly after the election, the vote tally showed McSally leading by more than 17,000 votes. However, it was soon reported[1] that not all votes had been counted and that there were still hundreds of thousands of early, provisional and out-of-precinct ballots that had not been counted. Those thousands of votes all favored the Democratic candidate. It therefore raised suspicions that the Republican candidate who supports Trump's agenda would have not only appeared to have won the race by only a slim margin, but actually slid well behind her Democratic challenger after additional ballots were counted once the election was over. A message from the Arizona Republican Party even went out requesting assistance with ballot counting and "ballot curing" (an authentication process that verifies the legitimacy of the signatures on ballots) after stating that the situation of new ballots coming in may easily "create an opening for corruption."

Stories detailing anomalies are common all across the United States. But, do those anomalies cross the line into criminal activity? Some advise never to attribute to malice what you can attribute to incompetence. Are there malicious actors intentionally and unduly influencing American elections? Are we able to determine if voter fraud is actually taking place in our country?

Indeed, there is evidence that election fraud does take place in the U.S., with instances of corruption going back to the 1700s. The largest ever voter fraud prosecution took place back in 1982 after an estimated 100,000 fraudulent votes were cast, which led to[2] 65 indictments and 61 convictions. But what about today?

My interest in writing a book on voter fraud stemmed from my own uncertainty about the integrity of our nation's elections, despite assurances from prominent people in both politics and media that widespread or large-scale election fraud isn't rampant. How would one know? No one has ever taken a comprehensive look. There are simply voices from both major political parties suggesting that the other side is gaming the system. We hear voices on the political Right alleging that the Left frequently attempts to steal elections and uses gerrymandering to assist in this goal. We hear voices on the political Left saying that the Right endorses voter ID laws as cover to suppress the voting power of minorities.

On May 11, 2017, shortly after taking office, President Trump signed an executive order creating the "Presidential Advisory Committee on Election Integrity." The Election Law Center supported the creation of the committee, saying[3], "Over the years, demonstrable and empirical data has been developed showing non-citizen voting, double voting and defects in the election system that no credible observer could deny."

But, not everyone shares this opinion.

After months of complaints and legal challenges from various states and special interest groups, President Trump was pressured into dissolving the group on January 3, 2018.

Key questions are raised by this outcome. Why would anyone object to an independent study of all 50 states of patterns and evidence that might indicate widespread fraud in our election and voting systems? Who wins and who loses from an exposé into election interference? Who objected to and presented legal challenges to uncovering potential fraud and abuse? Are allegations that exposing voter fraud would lead to voter suppression unfounded?

These questions as well as many others prompted me to pick up some of the slack and pursue my own journey of trying to answer questions of whether or not election fraud is real, and if so, how pervasive it may be.

I did not approach this book with preconceived notions about what I would or would not find. Clarity was my ultimate objective—not validating the beliefs of a particular political orthodoxy. What I discovered was disturbing and should motivate every single American to dig deeper into this issue and try to better understand the nuances of this topic, particularly as we head toward the 2020 election.

Buckle up. It's going to be a very bumpy ride.

Illegals Really Are Voting

"Every election is determined by the people
who show up."

— Larry J. Sabato

Rosa Ortega is a Mexican national who was arrested in Tarrant County, Texas[1] in 2016 for illegally voting five separate times in U.S. elections. Ortega took advantage of the weaknesses in our voting system, cast ballots and got caught. But, many other foreign nationals—who have no business voting in our elections—managed to fly under the radar. Ortega's story illustrates a fact that political operatives try to vehemently sweep under the rug, which is that illegal aliens are voting in United States elections. It is not a myth. It is not a false narrative. It is an empirical reality, and it is likely happening every election cycle.

Yet, the true extent of this problem cannot be easily

quantified, as there is no way to know exactly how many votes are being cast by and counted from illegal aliens. Think of it this way: roughly 93,000 speeding tickets are issued[2] each day across the U.S. Does that mean only 93,000 people were speeding? Certainly not. It means that only 93,000 people get caught. As evidenced by our own daily commutes to work, the number of speeding drivers is much higher than the number pulled over and cited for speeding. The same logic applies to voter fraud. With myriad loopholes available across all 50 states—that each establish their own election laws—it is next to impossible to know the exact number of illegals who are voting. Critics of tougher measures to better secure our elections often cite this blind spot as evidence that fraud is not taking place. Nothing could be further from the truth.

In Texas, where Ortega lived, knowingly voting illegally is a second-degree felony[3] that is punishable by up to 20 years in prison. Despite this, multiple people have been caught, tens of thousands of people are illegally registered to vote and, shockingly, some politicians both support and openly encourage this illegal behavior.

It is disingenuous to spend three years feigning outrage over the prospect of foreign interference in U.S. elections by Russia, only to turn a blind eye to actual election interference from foreign nationals living in our own country.

In 2015, Rasmussen survey data showed[4] that more than 53 percent of all Democrats thought that illegal aliens should be allowed to vote, and less than a quarter of Republicans thought that illegal aliens should be allowed to vote, while 35 percent of the U.S. population as a whole believed[5] illegals should be able to vote. These viewpoints reflect not only those of private citizens but are also widely shared by elected public officials. And support for illegals having the right to vote tends to fall squarely along party lines.

In 2018, the U.S. House of Representatives voted on H. Res 1071, a bill condemning illegal alien voting, which recognized[6] that "allowing illegal immigrants the right to vote devalues the franchise and diminishes the voting power of United States citizens." 140 Democrats refused[7] to support this bill, either voting against it or simply voting "present."

Dan Stein, President for the Federation for American Immigration Reform (FAIR) released a statement[8] on the resolution, saying:

> *"House Resolution 10718, which recognizes that allowing illegal immigrants the right to vote devalues the franchise and diminishes the voting power of United States citizens, was approved today in the House by a 279-72 vote, with 69 members simply voting present. Recently, a handful of local jurisdictions[9] including San Francisco, CA—which is mentioned specifically in the resolution— have begun to not only allow, but actively encourage, illegal aliens to vote in certain municipal elections.*
>
> *"Allowing illegal aliens to vote in elections at the local, state or federal level is a slap in the face to the American people because it diminishes their voices by elevating those*

of foreign nationals who are in the country illegally. Moreover, granting voting privileges to non-citizens before they've finished their naturalization process demeans citizenship and waters down the very thing which most immigrants seek and cherish.

"Unfortunately, this vote only further demonstrates that many Democrats in Congress are more concerned with their open borders agenda than they are with their fellow citizens."

Stein's words thoroughly sum this issue up. And, refusal to prevent—or even condemn—the practice of allowing non-citizen voting validates the attitudes of many Americans who believe that left-leaning policy makers don't truly take our voting rights seriously. The perception that Democrats/progressives are the party of open-borders and illegal immigration is reinforced through a sustained lack of empathy for Americans, particularly when it comes to guaranteeing that only legal U.S. citizens are able to vote. It's somewhat duplicitous to issue statements about the integrity and security of our elections when it comes to possible interference by the Russians (because you think they helped President Trump) while refusing to take meaningful action against verifiable interference by illegal aliens here at home (because you think they will help you).

The goal here is crystal clear: win at all costs. Disenfranchising U.S. citizens is merely seen as collateral damage and a completely acceptable cost to proponents of illegal aliens voting. And we have even more evidence of this fact.

On March 8, 2019, the U.S. House of Representatives—now led by Democrats—actually voted to defend[10] illegal aliens' right to vote in U.S. elections. This represents a complete 180-degree turn from the Republican-controlled House that condemned it just months prior. Rep John Lewis (D-Ga.) said[11], "We are prepared to open up the political process and let all of the people come in," even though illegal aliens voting is...well...illegal. Contrast that statement with a comment[12] from Rep. Dan Crenshaw (R-Texas) who asked, "What kind of government would cancel the vote of its own citizens, and replace it with non-citizens?" and you have a clear example of the ideological disparity between the two major American parties in 2019. Some Democrats have no qualms with promoting illegal voting and go out of their way to encourage ineligible voters to find their way to the polls on election day.

In 2014, Greg Amick, Campaign Manager for Mecklenburg County Sheriff candidate Irwin Carmichael was forced to resign, after hidden camera footage taken by Project Veritas (PV) shows him openly encouraging an illegal alien to vote. Amick asks if they have their driver's license and the person says they do, but added, "the only problem, you know, I don't want to vote if I'm not legal. I think that's going to be a problem. I'm not sure." Amick replied, "It won't be, it shouldn't be an issue at all." He added, "As long as you're registered to vote, you'll be fine. [13]"

It was reported[14] in November 2018 that Democrat activists were "issuing Spanish-language instructions to illegal aliens regarding how to vote" multiple times in U.S. elections. Not only were illegal aliens targeted and encouraged to vote, but lax policies regarding voter ID laws meant they would be able to cast multiple illegal ballots. This shows that not only is illegal voting taking place but it's also actively being facilitated. Much of the country is unaware of stories like this because, all too often, a sympathetic, lap dog, legacy media establishment either obfuscates or simply doesn't report this information.

For instance, despite video evidence showing former President Barack Obama openly encouraging[15] illegals to vote, a New York magazine ran an article[16] titled "Why So many People Believe Obama 'Encouraged' Illegals to Vote" wherein they described the videotaped incident as fake news. Quite the bit of irony.

In the interview, Obama was asked, "Many of the millennials, Dreamers, undocumented citizens—and I call them citizens because they contribute to this country—are fearful of voting. So if I vote, will Immigration know where I live? Will they come for my family and deport us?" Obama replied, "Not true, and the reason is, first of all, when you vote, you are a citizen yourself. And there is not a situation where the voting rolls somehow are transferred over and people start investigating, etc. The sanctity of the vote is strictly confidential."

In just a few words the then-sitting president of the United States said that casting an illegal ballot essentially circumvented the entire naturalization process and con-ferred U.S. citizenship to a foreign national. Also revealing was his admission that the voter rolls are a complete mess and unable to be adequately verified. Actions considered fraudulent are protected by the confidentiality of the vote, he surmised. Incredible language from a man who swore an oath to defend the citizens of this country, not foreigners who forced their way in. Obama's own words openly en-courage illegals to vote.

Many believe that this position is taken based on a belief that illegal aliens in this country will vote for Democrats. So, their hope is to expand the Democratic voting bloc by extending special favors to them. This idea couldn't be presented in a more transparent way than in a leaked memo written by Jennifer Palmieri, President of the Center for American Progress—a progressive think tank—which described[17] "Dreamers" of the Deferred Action for Childhood Arrivals (DACA) program as "a critical component of the Democratic Party's future electoral success." Party insiders don't hide the fact that they're using these people for votes. Even as far back as the presidential administration of Bill Clinton, his vice president, Al Gore, was tasked with[18] getting as many illegals as possible "sworn in as citizens, just in case the 1996 election turned out to be close." Part of the reason the Left opposes a border wall and a real fix for our immigration system is the same reason they turn a blind eye to illegal voting—a thirst for expanded power.

Palmieri isn't the only progressive operative who has suggested that illegal aliens are a major component to the future of the Democratic party. Eliseo Medina, an immigration adviser for Obama, not only expressed his desire to turn the United States into a single party state, he told[19] the Service Employees International Union that progressives need to be "solidly on the side of immigrants" in order to "solidify and expand the progressive coalition for the future." The goal was clear for Medina, a Communist Party USA supporter and former honorary chair of the Democratic Socialists of America. Progressives needed to capitalize on the influx of illegal aliens and convert them[20] into millions of new voters to "create a governing coalition for the long term, not just for an election cycle."

In hindsight, it's rather easy to see the pivot toward policies that favor illegal aliens. For instance, in 2006 and 2013 there were plenty of Democrats who supported legislation that would build and fund a wall on America's southern border. Fast forward to 2016 and such policies are considered racist and an affront to the brown people coming here to seek a better life. And, maybe these quasi-open borders policies are having their intended effect, because studies have found the following:

- In 2012, 62% of immigrants identified as Democrats, 25% as Republicans
- 81% of immigrant Latinos said they preferred "a bigger government providing more services"
- 76% of illegal aliens are Latinos

- 71% of Latinos voted for Barack Obama in 2012

So, with a supportive base that has graciously accepted the offer to remain a permanent underclass reliant on big government programs, it's no wonder Democrats are so energetically courting Latinos. For the same reason, they have no interest in curbing their voting, even if that voting is being done illegally.

And while there might still be some lackluster attempts to suggest that illegal voting isn't happening much or that we shouldn't worry about it, it's clear that it is happening frequently all around the country. But, discussions about exactly how many illegal aliens are voting always turn contentious. For instance, after President Trump won the 2016 election, Democrats fumed over having lost the presidency because President Trump won the Electoral College, despite the contention that they won the popular vote.

President Trump ignited a controversy (which still has not ended) when he tweeted[21], "In addition to winning the Electoral College in a landslide, I won the popular vote if you deduct the millions of people who voted illegally." This claim, while likely true, is difficult to prove because of (among other things) the decentralized nature of our election systems, the unwillingness of politicians to have real accountability and the cost of investigating fraud. But, the lack of a specific figure gave rise to the mainstream media's use of the term "without evidence" to qualify the president's statement on this issue and many others in a bid to discredit him, even though they have no evidence that he's wrong. Remember from my example about speeding tickets: just because a certain number are caught doesn't mean more aren't guilty.

In an article entitled "Without Evidence Donald Trump Says Millions of People Voted 'Illegally' in the Election He Won," Time reported[22] on President Trump's statement, saying, "There is no evidence that millions voted illegally." In a 2017 article from the notoriously anti-Trump newspaper *The New York Times*, the bias was first presented in a headline[23] reading "Trump Repeats Lie About Popular Vote in Meeting With Lawmakers" just before opening the piece with "President Trump used his first official meeting with congressional leaders on Monday to falsely claim that millions of unauthorized immigrants had robbed him of a popular vote majority, a return to his obsession with the election's results even as he seeks support for his legislative agenda." The piece went on to say that fact-checkers had judged the president's assertion as untrue. A more balanced assessment of the issue of illegal aliens voting reveals that the president was probably correct.

California Political Review reported on a 2015 study by Old Dominion/George Mason, which showed[24] "13 percent of noncitizen respondents admitted they were registered to vote, which matches closely [an] Old Dominion/George Mason study finding that 14.8 percent of noncitizens admitted they were registered to vote in 2008 and 15.6 percent of noncitizens admitted they were registered in 2010." Are we to expect that millions of illegal aliens are being encouraged to vote, are being promised by

Democrats in power that there won't be consequences, are taking the time to register to vote (or are conveniently registered automatically), but are just sitting at home on election day? The likelihood is that illegal aliens are indeed voting in greater numbers than we're told, and the impact they may have on electoral contests should not be understated.

Over the years, there have been varying estimates on the number of illegal aliens in the country. On the low end, Pew Research estimated the number at roughly 11 million. However, there are flaws associated with these numbers, in that the study failed to take into account anchor babies (of which there are at least 6.5 million) and political pressure likely results in actual numbers of illegals being suppressed.

On the high end, there are an estimated 30 million illegal aliens in the United States. This figure was notably cited[25] on MSNBC by Arturo Sarukhan, Mexico's former ambassador to the U.S. In the book Minutemen: The Battle to Secure America's Borders, it's also suggested that the number is around 30 million[26], but "by basing their estimates on flawed data, federal officials prefer a deliberate undercount that obscures the extent of the illegal immigration crisis." A study by Californians for Population Stabilization (CAPS) showed the number of illegal aliens in the U.S. to potentially be as high as 38 million. And, conservative author and speaker Ann Coulter estimated the number of illegals in the country to be closer to 30 million. She based her findings[27] on "banking and remittance payment records, government service demands (like how many immigrants were applying for driver's licenses), and arrests by the U.S. Department of Immigration and Customs Enforcement (ICE)." And, although critics dismissed the findings as "baseless," an Ivy League university study lends weight to the higher—more controversial—estimate.

A recent study from Yale University[28] also showed the number could be as high as 30 million, but settled on an estimated 22.1 million illegal aliens in the country. The *Yale Daily News* reported[29] in 2018:

> *"Researchers at the Yale School of Management have estimated the number of undocumented immigrants in the United States to be nearly twice as large as the number widely accepted and extrapolated from the Census Bureau's annual American Community Survey.*
>
> *"The study, conducted by Yale professors Jonathan Feinstein and Edward Kaplan as well as MIT lecturer Mohammad Fazel-Zarandi, used demographic modeling data to produce a range of 16.2 million to 29.5 million undocumented immigrants in the U.S., with an average estimate of 22.1 million. The study was published on Sept. 21 in the journal PLOS One.*
>
> *"This number—22.1 million—stands in contrast to the widely accepted estimate of 11.3 million, a number frequently referenced by politicians in recent elections."*

Here's why it matters: rather than using the higher (more likely) estimate, let's just accept the very conservative estimate above that shows that 13 percent of illegals admit to being registered to vote in our elections. If 13 percent of a population of 22.1 million actually voted, it would mean that, in the 2016 presidential election, the number of ballots cast by illegal aliens would have been at least 2.8 million— the exact same margin by which Hillary Clinton is said to have supposedly beaten President Trump in the popular vote. If the illegal population is actually 30 million and 13 percent voted, it would put the illegal alien ballots cast at 3.9 million. This doesn't take into account the fact that only 13 percent *admitted* to being registered to vote illegally. If we account for those who won't admit to it, the actual number of illegals voting could be substantially higher.

Some claim to have debunked these numbers. A New Jersey research group called Just Facts, an independent think tank, examined the data "from an extensive Harvard/YouGov study" and confronted "both sides in the illegal voting debate: those who say[30] it happens a lot and those who say the problem is nonexistent."

The other side of this coin are professors who contend that zero illegal aliens vote. But, as the *Washington Times* reported, "the liberal mainstream media adopted this position and proclaimed the Old Dominion work 'debunked.'"

The report continued: "The ODU professors, who stand by their work in the face of attacks from the Left, concluded that in 2008, as few as 38,000 and as many as 2.8 million noncitizens voted." It also said the think tank's "analysis of the same polling data settled on much higher numbers. He estimated that as many as 7.9 million noncitizens were illegally registered that year and 594,000 to 5.7 million voted."

If that many noncitizens really voted back in 2008, and the country took in millions more illegal aliens under the Obama administration, it is likely that more than 5.7 million illegal aliens voted in 2016. (*Note: this estimate does not take into account other forms of illegal voting done by U.S. citizens. More on this later.*)

Still think Hillary actually won the popular vote? To the dismay of progressives, the data bolster the legitimacy of President Trump's statements.

Thank God for the Electoral College.

The impact of illegal aliens on elections isn't just limited to direct voting. In the last presidential election, the Left was hoping the illegal vote could carry Hillary Clinton into the White House. *Politico* actually ran a piece[31] with the headline "Illegal Immigrants Could Elect Hillary: How noncitizens decrease Republican chances of winning the White House next year." The piece stated "illegal immigrants—along with other non-citizens without the right to vote—may pick the 2016 presidential winner," fully admitting that illegal aliens being counted in the census gives states with sanctuary policies and high populations of illegal aliens additional electoral college votes and can swing an election to the Left. This was based on a conservative estimate of only 11 million illegal aliens being in the country. Estimates of illegals potentially as high as 30 million and (as of April 2019) 100,000 illegal aliens per month pouring across our border lends credence to the idea of adding the citizenship question back to our census and beginning to take serious steps toward verifying exactly how many people are in our country illegally.

Eric Eggers, in his book, *Fraud: How the Left Plans to Steal the Next Election*, further explained the impact that illegal aliens have on our electorate, even if they're not casting votes. He wrote:

> *"...noncitizens could tip the balance in a close general election because, just as their inclusion in the Census inflates a state's population, so too does it inflate that state's number of electoral votes. California, now a sanctuary state, is the biggest beneficiary of extra federal representation. Using 2010 Census data—and the number of immigrants, legal and illegal, has grown dramatically since then—[Professor Leonard] Steinhorn calculated that California would lose five House seats and New York and Washington State would each lose one congressional seat without their noncitizen populations. In other words, noncitizens in Washington and New York offset the voting power in the House of Representatives of the citizens of Alaska, Montana, North Dakota, South Dakota, Wyoming, Vermont, and Delaware, all of which have one House member, and the noncitizens of California offset the representation of citizens in the twenty-four states that have five or fewer representatives in the House."*

Eggers said, "That is not electoral fraud *per se*, but it underlines the point that elections in the United States are determined by more factors than legal voting." The fact that there are large numbers of illegal aliens registered to vote (with an unknown number of them actually voting) and counted in the Census should be a cause for concern for every American.

Somehow, many Americans never hear of this type of data. If they do, what they hear is misleading, as proponents of change and oversight on this issue usually have their statements offset by claims of racism and voter suppression. There are incredible disinformation campaigns run against people who discuss the likelihood of these cases of fraud, with headlines like this one written by the *Washington Post*[32]: "Lou Dobbs Casually Makes Up Story That 'Many' Illegal Immigrants Voted in Midterms and Had 'Immense Impact.'" Let me breakdown the headline for you.

- "Casually": as in, this was an afterthought and he's spent no time seriously weighing the merits of this issue.
- "Makes up" = he's lying.
- 'Many' illegal immigrants voted: the quotes imply the opposite, which is that few illegals voted (again suggesting he's lying)
- 'Immense impact': the quotes suggest there's little to no impact when illegals vote

Misleading headlines like this are not written by accident. Writers and editors have access to a considerable amount of information on this topic. They make conscious decisions to ignore it and mislead their readers. Publishers know that many people only skim headlines and most don't read all the way through full articles. The *Post* even once cited[33] research showing that 59 percent of people share news links on social media without ever actually reading the story. For many readers, a headline like the one trashing Lou Dobbs becomes gospel because they will never read a word beyond it.

Those who make it through these delusory hit pieces will quickly realize that the article was not published to inform voters but to personally attack the character of someone guilty of nothing more than presenting unpopular information. Dobbs in no way made up these stories. And, at no point did the *Post* refute Dobbs' claim or present contradictory evidence to justify such an incendiary headline.

In the run-up to the 2018 midterms, Georgia gubernatorial candidate Stacey Abrams said[34] that the expected blue wave was "comprised of those who are documented and undocumented." She, as a candidate for governor, publicly suggested that illegal aliens not only *might* be voting but were *expected* to be voting. Her candor suggests this practice is considered acceptable within progressive circles. And, although she also said that she did not need "conservative values" to win[35], she clearly believed she and other candidates did not need American votes to win either; an ethos that surely has permeated other parts of the country where illegal voting is clearly taking place.

In 2014, an NBC reporter located dozens of illegals

who were actively voting in Florida in "vast numbers." In the report, it is noted that it's difficult to know the pervasiveness of the problem because illegals aren't able to be tracked. Guy Benson of *Townhall* reported on this story.

"WBBH-TV reporter Andy Pierrotti managed to track down dozens[36] of local residents who were (a) both non-U.S. citizens and (b) registered to vote in the swing state. Many of them had illegally voted in recent elections," he wrote[37]. He continued: "We don't know how widespread this problem is because elections offices don't keep track of where non-citizens live. So we decided to do something that they'd never tried to do before: We found them on our own."

The investigation began by examining state forms on which residents had declined jury duty by checking a box indicating that they weren't U.S. citizens, and were therefore ineligible to serve. Pierrotti then cross-referenced those results with local voter rolls, identifying at least 94 people who were illegally registered to vote in the state of Florida. Next, he visited some of these people at their homes, where they admitted that they weren't citizens and professed ignorance as to how they were registered to vote in the first place. But, voting records confirmed that they'd exercised their "right" to vote—a right that, as non-citizens, they do not actually possess.

In 2018, a study in New Jersey found that hundreds of non-citizens were registered to vote. However, not only were they registered to vote, local officials knew they were in the country illegally when they granted them voting privileges. *PJ Media* reported[38], "three-quarters of the non-citizens had revealed their ineligible status to a New Jersey state official, who then presented and accepted the illegal forms anyway." the study, conducted by the Public Interest Legal Foundation (PILF), found[39]:

> *"The apparent cause of the situation is a consequence of requirements enacted by a federal law: former President Bill Clinton's National Voter Registration Act of 1993, commonly known as "Motor Voter." Under "Motor Voter," state officials are required to offer voter registration forms and to ask citizens if they would like to register during certain interactions. Per the law's nickname, this most often occurs during a citizen's visit to a Department of Motor Vehicles.*

> *"However, officials in New Jersey—and likely throughout the country—have been presenting voter registration forms to non-citizens.*

> *"And in the vast majority of the cases found by the study, this was not accidental: most non-citizens revealed their ineligible status—some even presented green cards—yet were given the forms anyway."*

This study found that government officials are knowingly giving foreign nationals credentials needed to vote in U.S. elections. To put a finer point on this, it means that state and local officials are colluding with foreign nationals in an effort to influence an election.

Not everyone is on board with this program. In an op-ed for savejersey.com, Matt Rooney explained what many see as the real motivation behind this, writing[40], "This isn't about justice. It's about power, and there is power in numbers. They're working overtime to guarantee that legal, taxpaying residents are soon outnumbered by residents who aren't legal, aren't paying, and are therefore natural allies for [Democrats]."

The push to normalize illegal aliens voting is happening all around the country. Drivers licenses are usually acceptable forms of identification for the purposes of casting a ballot. States that currently issue[41] driver's licenses to illegals are California, Colorado, Connecticut, Delaware, Hawaii, Illinois, Maryland, New Mexico, Nevada, Utah, Vermont, Washington and the District of Columbia.

Chicago, Illinois recently issued hundreds of thousands of municipal ID cards, a new government-issued state ID. And, while it may be used as an alternate for a public library card or CTA Ventra fare card, the CityKey program that created this card has another purpose. "The Illinois Election Code requires the Board of Elections to accept current, valid photo identification cards and other local governmental documentation that includes an individual's name and address, as proof of identity and residency," said Anna Valencia[42], who leads the program. "The CityKey fits both of these requirements." Chicago officials are well-aware that illegals are voting, given that there have already been people arrested and charged[43] with misrepresenting their citizenship in order to illegally cast a ballot.

This program alone has the potential to illegally add hundreds of thousands (maybe millions) of non-citizens to Illinois voter rolls—which is exactly the point. By pushing state issued IDs for foreign nationals, Mayor Rahm Emanuel was proactively getting ahead of any effort to institute voter ID laws by simply issuing photo identification to people who are here illegally. Any future effort to screen voter eligibility based on whether or not someone had government ID would be useless without going through additional, cumbersome and politically risky steps.

It's important to note that, although there are many jurisdictions that facilitate illegals voting, there are some officials who still uphold U.S. law. In 2019, Michael Kearns, Erie County Clerk (New York), responded to new legislation passed by the state that allowed illegal aliens to apply for driver's licenses. He vowed to not issue licenses to non-citizens, even though it had become state law. "This is very important. This is not only about the law, but security and voter fraud," he told[44] Fox & Friends. "In the auto bureaus in New York, people can register to vote and there was a discussion on the assembly and Senate floor, the sponsors of the bill said there are already people in New York who are voting illegally."

He also dispelled the myth that illegal aliens aren't committing voter fraud. "I don't buy that because we know, I spoke with ICE and one of the things they told me and conveyed to me is that when they apprehend people who are here illegally, one of the forms of identification they have is a voter card," he told Fox.

New York certainly isn't an anomaly.

A 2016 investigation by the Public Interest Legal Foundation found[45] that in Virginia, using a sample of only eight counties (not including Fairfax and Arlington counties), there were nearly 1,046 non-citizens who were registered to vote. Extrapolating those figures across the entire state, we would expect to see more than 12,400 illegal aliens registered to vote in Virginia. It's nearly impossible to get an accurate picture of what's really happening here because, as PILF states, "Virginia state election officials are obstructing access to public records that reveal the extent to which non-citizens are participating in our elections." The fact of the matter is that they are aiding and abetting criminals.

According to *The Washington Times*[46], the noncitizens were caught accidentally, only because when they renewed their driver's licenses, they inadvertently revealed to authorities that they were not here legally.

It is a felony when an illegal alien completes a voter registration form. PILF outlines a list of laws that are broken the moment a non-citizen registers to vote in Virginia:

> *"The offenses a fraudulent voter might commit when he registers and votes are numerous:*
> *Virginia Code § 24.2-1004: Criminalizes casting an illegal ballot.*
>
> *Title 18, United States Code § 611: Criminalizes voting by illegal aliens in federal elections.*

Title 18, United States Code § 911: Criminalizes representing oneself to be a citizen of the United States.

Title 18, United States Code § 1015: Criminalizes false statements in order to register to vote or to vote in any Federal, State, or local election.

Title 52, United States Code § 20511: Criminalizes the fraudulent submission of voter registration applications and the fraudulent casting of ballots."

The Federal for American Immigration Reform (FAIR) lists two additional federal statutes that prohibit illegal voting:

• *Pursuant to 8 U.S.C. § 1227, any alien who has voted in violation of any Federal, State, or local constitutional provision, statute, ordinance, or regulation is deportable.*

• *Pursuant to 42 U.S.C. § 1973gg-10(2) any false statement concerning an applicant's citizenship status that is made on a registration form submitted to election authorities is a crime.*

Virginia is also a state that takes advantage of the National Voter Registration Act, which allows states to register people to vote based on their having a driver's license. There is no requirement for states to verify citizenship. The registrant simply has to "swear under penalty of perjury" that they are a citizen and, voilà, they may begin to cancel out the votes of actual citizens.

So accepted is the Democrats' support for illegal aliens voting that in 2014 the *Washington Post* aided them and actually published[47] a chart showing which states do and do not require identification. Writer Marc Wachtler said that the chart[48] identifying states with lax voting laws provided a blueprint for illegal voting and "thanks to radical racial groups like La Raza and Asian Americans Advancing Justice, the *Post's* hand-out is turning up amid voting instructions for illegal immigrants who aren't legally able to vote but who will be among the millions of voters casting ballots Tuesday anyway."

California, a sanctuary state, has some of the most laissez-faire policies toward illegal voting. Illegal aliens are now officially allowed to vote in San Francisco. Proposition N passed in 2016, paving the way for non-citizens to cast ballots and contribute to re-shaping the state. *NBC News* reported[49] that San Francisco allows illegal aliens to vote in school board elections, "following a handful of other municipalities that have opened up local elections to noncitizens."

Also, in 2018, it was reported[50] that California would begin automatically "registering adults who obtain or renew a driver's license to vote, leading to some concern noncitizens and immigrants illegally living in the state could find it easier to cast ballots in elections." Concern came from a new extension of the California Motor Voter Act that would send state driver information to voter rolls.

The report also said:

"You're setting the state up for a disaster. They don't seem to have a process in place to verify that people are who they say they are. It's a free-for-all, a process that can be manipulated," said Catherine Engelbrecht, *founder of True the Vote, a national organization that unsuccessfully pressed Gov. Jerry Brown to veto the law allowing automatic registration.*

"A California official pushed back against those concerns, telling Fox News those who must apply for or renew a special license classification – the AB 60, named after the bill that gave illegals the right to apply for licenses in 2015 - would be excluded from the voter notification process.

"The driver license application program prevents undocumented Californians from being able to register to vote," said Jessica Gonzalez, *Assistant Deputy Director of the DMV.*

"Automatic programming will not let them go to the (voter) registration section. It will be automatically grayed out and can't be bypassed. It will require proof of U.S. citizenship and California residency."

But who's to say that the system is not able to be bypassed? Who can say that at some point in the future it won't be altered in a way that allows someone to circumvent safe-guards or that those safeguards will be later abandoned entirely?

And, we do have clear examples of the dangers of such lax policies because, it was reported that, California's automatic voter registration system "led to double-registering as many as 77,000[51]" people. It also erroneously registered more than 23,000[52] people, according to the *LA Times*. Somehow these failures haven't seemed to call into question the feasibility of auto-registration. And state officials aren't too concerned. After all, California is a state that maintains millions of ineligible names on its voter rolls and fights tooth and nail to avoid purging them. Its preference for illegals over citizens is already codified in its numerous sanctuary policies and refusal to assist federal agents in detaining and deporting convicted criminal aliens.

In Colorado, a study found[53] that 5,000 illegal aliens voted as far back as the 2010 election. *The Hill* reported that Colorado's Secretary of State Scott Gessler said his department identified almost 12,000 noncitizens who were registered to vote and nearly 5,000 who actually participated in the election. "A disturbing wake-up call" were the words Rep Gregg Harper (R-Miss.) used to describe the study. He told *The Hill*, "We simply cannot have an electoral system that allows thousands of non-citizens to violate the law and vote in our elections. We must do more to protect the integrity of our electoral processes."

It is also interesting that in 2017 hundreds of Colorado residents suddenly began cancelling their voter registrations after President Trump launched his commission to look into voter fraud. When it was announced that the federal government would be requesting data from states on their voter rolls to ensure election integrity, 472 people in Denver cancelled their registrations[54] as did 329 voters in Boulder County. "In order to conduct transparent and verifiable elections, the voter rolls must be publicly available to anyone," wrote Hillary Hall[55] in an op-ed. "Without voter registration and vote history being public there would be no way for any outside individual or organization to independently verify our election processes. It would simply have to be a 'trust us' scenario with your state or local elected official maintaining the voter rolls with no external oversight." That is the exact system we have now—one with little or no oversight—and it's created a dysfunction where illegal aliens vote and officials are able to mysteriously produce thousands of "found" ballots days after the polls have closed.

Pennsylvania is its own voter fraud horror show. Author and Political Commentator David Harris Jr. reported[56] that "There are currently 100,000 illegal aliens registered to vote in Pennsylvania, thanks to a previous Democrat law that automatically registered people when they renewed their driver's licenses," citing PILF. "Their information could be more complete, except the Democrat administration in the state has refused to give them information deemed to be public."

As we will see later on, the issues concerning voter rolls, refusal to turn over public information for the purpose of safeguarding elections is a common practice, including in the hotly contested swing state Pennsylvania.

Harris also cited a report, which noted several instances[57] of illegal aliens (who were registered Democrats) repeatedly gaming the Pennsylvania system:

> *"One man, Felipe Rojas-Orta, canceled his registration last year, filing a handwritten note saying he was not a citizen. He had, however, registered as a Democrat and voted in three separate elections, including most recently 2016, the year of the presidential race.*
>
> *"A woman had her registration canceled in 2006 as a noncitizen, yet re-registered to vote twice — and cast ballots in some elections. That woman, a registered Democrat, is still active in the system, the lawsuit says.*
>
> *"Yet another woman voted in 2008 and 2012, had her registration canceled in 2014 because she wasn't a citizen, then re-registered and voted in 2016, according to documents filed in court. She was registered as a Democrat."*

Politico reported[58] that President Trump won Pennsylvania by a tight margin of 68,236 votes. Can anyone say with certainty that the 100,000 illegally registered voters in Pennsylvania didn't cast ballots in that election? Was the margin actually that tight or did it include illegal votes? Even assuming that margin represents only legal voters, just three quarters of the illegal voters on the rolls could have handed that state to Hillary Clinton. Maybe illegal votes actually handed it to Trump. We will never know. But these are questions that shouldn't have to be raised. The mere possibility that foreign nationals can so easily swing a U.S. election should be cause for bipartisan concern across the country. And, we see officials in many states willing to simply overlook these startling facts while simultaneously declaring voter fraud to be a myth. Pennsylvania is one of those states.

In February 2019, *One News Now* reported that Pennsylvania Democrat Governor Tom Wolfe had finally acknowledged the illegal aliens on the state's voter rolls after legal action was taken. "I'm not surprised," Diane Gramley, president of the American Family Association of Pennsylvania, said[59]. "The entire situation is evident that Governor Wolfe has been attempting to hide the illegal registration of illegal aliens." Gov. Wolfe was leading the state in 2017 when it announced that it had no intention to participate in President Trump's election fraud task force, characterizing it as (you guessed it) a "systematic effort to suppress the vote." But, in the face of new evidence of widespread fraud throughout the state, it is clear that the lack of transparency in Pennsylvania has safeguarded bad actors and reliably increased the chances of fraudulent voting taking place.

Americans for Legal Immigration (ALI)[60] reported that just prior to the 2016 election, Pennsylvania "sent 2.5 million voter registration forms out to its registered drivers who had not yet registered to vote to implore them to sign up to cast their ballot in November." ALI also stated, "Many of those who received the registration cards turned out to not be American citizens, and therefore, are ineligible to vote." This swing state—with many in power being in staunch opposition to then-candidate Trump—sending out millions of voter registration forms right before an election to a group of people they absolutely knew included illegal voters is a strong sign that voter fraud is not only tolerated but also encouraged. It's difficult to imagine that this was simply an oversight, because a clear pattern of disregard that has been established in this state.

Additionally, measures to provide transparency and accountability have been shunned. The state's reluctance to allow examination of its voter rolls (coupled with documented cases of tens of thousands of names of ineligible voters) suggests that one, fraud is indeed taking place and two, the state has no interest in stopping it.

Pivoting back to the South, Ken Paxton, the Texas Attorney General, said[61] that the Texas Secretary of State discovered 95,000 non-citizens who are registered to vote in Texas and that roughly 58,000 of them are actually voting in Texas elections. *The New York Times* reported that the findings were the result[62] "of an 11-month investigation with the Texas Department of Public Safety that also found that about 58,000 people on the list had voted since 1996."

The New York Times stated that Democrats were skeptical of the impact of the claim because the 58,000 illegal votes would only have amounted to 0.69% of all votes that were cast. Just as we see in other states across the country, however, there are races that are decided by tight margins.

According to *Politico*[63], in the 2018 midterm election Republican Dan Crenshaw scored 139,188 votes while his Democrat challenger Todd Litton received 119,992—a margin of only 19,196 votes. Illegal votes could easily have swung this election and resulted in one fewer Republican in the House. In Texas's 3rd Congressional district, GOP candidate Van Taylor defeated Lorie Burch by a margin of 31,286 votes. The 10th congressional district between GOP candidate Michael McCaul and democrat Mike Siegel was decided by only 13,132 votes. We could go on and on, but the point is clear. In races across the country, elections are often won in margins smaller than the number of illegally registered voters.

The suggestion that illegal aliens are not voting across the country in large numbers is blatantly false because we have the data that shows otherwise. We know it's happening. Some people acknowledge it and others try to shut down the conversation. But Americans who actually care about the sanctity of the vote need to shift their focus to determining what action steps we can take to minimize illegal voting. Corrupt politicians and activists fight to prevent transparency and an accurate accounting of the problem. Every illegal ballot cast effectively cancels out the vote of a U.S. citizen. This is unacceptable in our constitutional republic.

Anomalies & Fraud in the 2018 Midterm Elections

"Those who vote decide nothing. Those who count the votes decide everything."

—*Joseph Stalin*

Midterm elections in the United States are held two years after the four-year Presidential election. There are multiple offices up for election during the midterm cycle including Congressional seats and some governorships. Occasionally, special elections are held during this cycle.

The 2018 midterm cycle was of particular importance. President Trump stunned the world with an unexpected victory in 2016 and had been mired in controversy over allegations that his campaign had colluded with the Russian government to help him win. That year, Republicans also won both chambers of Congress: the House and the Senate. In 2018, Democrats were eager to re-take control of Congress in order to try and launch an effort either to impeach or to otherwise remove the president from office. Additionally, during the first two years of its stewardship over the country, the Trump administration obliterated most of the legacy of America's previous President, Barack Hussein Obama.

From ending the Iran deal to pulling out of the Trans-Pacific Partnership and cutting regulations on departments including the Environmental Protection Agency, President Trump's policies erased much of his predecessor's legacy like shaking an Etch-a-sketch. In December 2016, President Trump was asked[1] about his plans and whether or not he would be taking a wrecking ball to Obama's legacy. President Trump said, "No, no, no. I don't want to do that at all. I just want what's right. On the EPA, you can't get things approved. People are waiting in line for 15 years before they get rejected, okay. That's why people don't want to invest in this country. You look at what's going on—and you can look at a jobs report, but take a look at the real jobs report, which are the millions of people that gave up looking for work, and they're not considered in that number that's less than 5 percent."

Despite tepid assurances that his motivations weren't political retaliation, Democrats were furious with President Trump's policy priorities—so much so that a *Huffington Post* contributor ironically ended a column[2] with the words "nothing you do or say... no amount of executive orders you sign... can erase the memory and legacy of one of America's most beloved and successful presidents. But keep trying. It just makes you appear smaller and smaller every minute of every day." The Left was completely indignant, and heading into the 2018 midterms there was but one clear objective: win enough seats to be able to try and remove the president from office.

Contributing to the heightened emotions of the election cycle was the fact that allegations were circulating that illegal activities had taken place during the tenure of the prior administration and were being investigated by the Trump administration. It was reported[3] in March 2018 that then-U.S. Attorney General Jeff Sessions brought on U.S. Attorney John Huber to conduct an investigation into possible criminal activity that took place during the Obama administration. Staffed with a team of 470 people, Huber was said to have the ability to empanel a grand jury and file criminal charges "anywhere, which means that it could be a group of citizens from deep-red Utah—in the heart of Trump country—instead of the D.C. Swamp that decides whether to hand down indictments for felony prosecution." Huber's powers were expected to exceed by a great margin those of any special counsel. His investigations, along with investigations by FBI Inspector General Michael Horowitz and Republican-led Congressional investigations looking into possible abuses, could have resulted (were they true) in the arrest, trial and sentencing of multiple Obama-era officials. But, if Democrats were able to retake control of Congress, they would have been able to shut down some of these investigations to protect their allies.

Against this backdrop, it was clear that much was at stake. This was no normal election.

Ultimately, the 2018 midterm elections descended into chaos after multiple states had anomalies and fraud allegations. The states with the most publicized irregularities in 2018 were Florida, Arizona and Georgia.

FLORIDA—PALM BEACH COUNTY

Two counties in Florida have found themselves repeatedly embroiled in controversy, resulting from their knack for consistently producing questionable election results. After the 2018 midterms in Palm Beach County—arguably one of the most corrupt counties in the U.S. for election fraud—Democrats pushed to count the votes of non-citizens. *The Federalist* reported[4] that during a review of provisional ballots to determine if a recount was needed in the Florida governor, senate, and agriculture commission races, Palm Beach County Supervisor of Elections Susan Bucher identified a voter as a non-citizen and declared that the ballot would not be counted. Attorneys representing the Democratic candidate for Senate Bill Nelson and the Democratic candidate for governor Andrew Gillum objected.

The Federalist reached out to Chairman of the Palm Beach County Republican Party Michael Barnett to verify that the exchange took place. "I would think this is something we could all agree on—that non-citizens shouldn't vote, but evidently that's not the case with Democrats,"

Barnett said. "It's really sad that we are having to deal with this in a close election. It just goes to show the depths they will go to in order to win."

Though the election took place on a Tuesday, by Friday afternoon Palm Beach County was one of two Florida counties that had not completed counting absentee ballots. State law requires[5] the canvassing board to "report all early voting and all tabulated vote-by-mail results to the Department of State within 30 minutes after the polls close."

Additionally, Palm Beach County prevented party officials from being present during the vote counting. They also magically produced an additional 15,000 ballots after the polls closed[6], which immediately raised suspicions because as journalist John Hayward wrote[7], "mysterious boxes of votes discovered after Election Day always seem to favor the Democrats by lopsided margins."

Florida Governor Rick Scott filed a lawsuit[8] against Palm Beach County, characterizing the way they handled the counting of the votes as "a clear violation of Florida law." The lawsuit cites Section 101.5614(4)(a), Fla. Stat., the provision of the Florida Election Code, which says (in part):

> *"If any vote by mail ballot is physically damaged so that it cannot properly be counted by the automatic tabulating equipment, a true duplicate copy shall be made of the damaged ballot in the presence of witnesses and substituted for the damaged ballot. Likewise, a duplicate ballot shall be made of a vote by mail ballot containing an over*

> *voted race or a marked vote by mail ballot in which every*
> *race is under voted which shall include all valid votes as*
> *determined by the canvassing board based on rules adopted*
> *by the division pursuant to s. 102.166(4)."*

The Supervisor of Elections made copies of ballots without the presence of witnesses to unilaterally decide which ballots were valid and which were not, a power which belongs exclusively to the canvassing board. The complaint states that the Supervisor of Elections was in clear violation of the law for:

- Refusing to allow representatives to properly witness the processing and duplication of physically damaged absentee ballots
- Not allowing representatives to properly witness staff review and processing of the ballots
- Denying access to roughly 1,500 faxed-in military ballots when they were converted to a standard ballot
- Disallowing the Palm Beach County Canvassing Board its statutory duty to determine "all valid votes" from absentee ballots

What happened in Palm Beach County could easily be attributed to malice and described as fraud. The actions taken by state election officials exceeded the threshold of incompetence or disregard. Common sense would suggest that finding thousands of ballots that were missing on election day and processing those ballots behind closed doors would raise suspicions. Yet, optics be damned, election officials decided to proceed anyway, in violation of state law.

President Trump offered his own criticism of the Florida vote count effort, tweeting that an "honest vote count is no longer possible." He also expressed concern that "new ballots showed up out of nowhere," adding to suspicions that improprieties were taking place.

In her defense, Bucher cited racism as the reason for accusations of questionable behavior. Townhall.com reported[9] that Bucher responded to the criticism from President Trump, Gov. Rick Scott, and Sen. Marco Rubio by calling it "unfortunate," and said Republicans were "trying to disrupt our democracy because they don't like the demographics of our voters." However, based on violations of Florida law, criticism of her actions was justified. *Townhall* writer Matt Vespa wrote, "According to Title IX, Chapter 102 of the 2018 Florida Statutes, she isn't doing her job. The law stipulates that all early voting and all vote-by-mail results be reported to the Department of State within 30 minutes after the polls close. This did not happen. Instead, three days after Election Day, no one even knows how many votes are left to be counted."

This is not the first time Palm Beach County has come under fire for questionable elections practices. This county, along with Florida's Broward County, has a history of disputed vote tallies.

In 2016, incumbents Bruce Guyton and Lynne Hubbard were running against each other in a contest for city council. *CBS News* reported[10] that "after a recount of the March 29 runoff election, Guyton and Hubbard wound up with an equal number of votes." On the other hand, the *Palm Beach Post* noted that "a day before the recount, Palm Beach County Elections Supervisor Susan Bucher found[11] 18 uncounted absentee ballots on a shelf." Allegations of voter fraud abounded, and a lawsuit was filed, as several of the absentee ballots were cast by three of Hubbard's relatives.

The same year, Democrat state senate candidate Bobby Powell was accused of vote tampering through a practice known as "ballot brokering." This practice is usually done in minority neighborhoods and is conducted by going door-to-door to try and influence voters to vote for a certain candidate. However, the practice is illegal because the broker usually ends up completing the absentee ballot for the voter rather than the voter casting the ballot himself.

FLORIDA - BROWARD COUNTY

While the issues in Palm Beach County are concerning, Broward has its own set of challenges when it comes to potential election meddling. Arguably the most troubled county in the country when it comes to allegations of election fraud, Broward County has been rocked with scandal after scandal following its handling of the 2018 midterms. The Supervisor of Elections in this county was Brenda Snipes, a woman with a history of shady dealings that goes back more than a decade. Many question exactly how she's continued to get elected and how she's been able to insulate herself from being fired and brought up on criminal charges in light of her checkered past. *Politico* wrote[12], "Snipes has been involved in so many snafus that the *Miami Herald* published a story on her agency four days before the midterms titled 'Inside the Most Controversial Elections Department in Florida.'"

Broward County's 2018 woes began right after the election. On the night of the election, the Broward County Supervisor of Elections Office said[13] 634,000 votes had been cast. However, provisional and mail-in ballots popped-up out of nowhere, and by Thursday the total vote count was up to 712,040. Remember, Florida law requires all provisional and mail-in ballots to be counted by the night of the election and reported within thirty minutes of the polls closing. Snipes failed to provide an accurate count of exactly how many ballots they had in their possession and failed to report the chain-of-custody of those ballets (in other words, who had possession of them and where they were located).

For days, multiple ballots continued to materialize out of thin air. Alarming to most people across the nation was that every single ballot increased the tally for Democrats only. *Not a single ballot was produced that worked in favor of Republicans.*

Sen. Marco Rubio (R-Fla.) tweeted[14], "[Florida] law requires counties report early voting & vote-by-mail within 30 minutes after polls close. 43 hours after polls closed 2 Democrat strongholds [Broward County] & [Palm Beach

County] are still counting & refusing to disclose how many ballots they have left to count." The unwillingness of Snipes to provide an accurate accounting of ballot processing raised suspicions that fraud was taking place.

National Republican Senatorial Committee and Rick Scott for Senate sued Snipes, stating in their court filing[15]:

> *"Two days after voting has concluded, the Supervisor Of Elections is unwilling to disclose records revealing how many electors voted, how many ballots have been canvassed, and how many ballots remain to be canvassed. The lack of transparency raises substantial concerns about the validity of the election process. An emergency hearing is necessary as the Canvassing Board is obligated to submit the unofficial elections results to the Division of Elections by noon, November 10, 2018. A recount in at least two, possibly three, of the statewide races appears likely."*

The lawsuit also said:

- *that the [National Republican Senatorial Committee and Scott, per Florida law] have the right to inspect or copy any public record made or received in connection with the official business of any public body, officer or employee of the state, or persons acting on their behalf, except with respect to records exempted pursuant to this section or specifically made confidential by this Constitution.*
- *Every person who has custody of a public record shall permit the record to be inspected and copied by any person desiring to*

> *do so, at any reasonable time, under reasonable conditions, and under supervision by the custodian of the public records.*

- *When ballots are produced under this section for inspection or examination, no persons other than the supervisor of elections or the supervisor's employees shall touch the ballots. If the ballots are being examined before the end of the contest period in s. 102.168, the supervisor of elections shall make a reasonable effort to notify all candidates by telephone or otherwise of the time and place of the inspection or examination. All such candidates, or their representatives, shall be allowed to be present during the inspection or examination.*

Despite the fact that Snipes was legally obligated to allow witnesses to supervise the ballots and vote counting, she simply ignored requests to do so. The lawsuit also says that Snipes failed to provide information on exactly how many ballots were cast, how many ballots were counted and how many ballots were remaining to be counted, in violation of Florida law.

A judge ordered a mandatory recount of all the votes, which was to take place using machines that would re-scan and re-count all ballots. The Tuesday after the election, Elections Supervisor Brenda Snipes assured everyone that Broward would not miss Thursday's deadline. "We will complete the recount," she said[16]. "There has never been a deadline we have missed." The results of the recount needed to be in two days later, by 3pm on November 15.

Despite Snipes' assurances, election officials did miss the deadline by just two minutes, which prompted immediate allegations of fraud since it was learned shortly afterward that the recount would have actually increased Republican Ron DeSantis's lead over Democrat Andrew Gillum in the race for governor by 755 votes, while Republican Gov. Scott's lead could have been increased by 779 votes[17].

A local reporter for *The New York Times* said[18] the county "finished on time," but the election workers claimed they submitted late because of "unfamiliarity with the state website."

"We uploaded to the state two minutes late so the state has chosen not to use our machine recount results and they are going to use the first unofficial results as our second unofficial results," state election worker Joe D'Alessandro said[19]. The canvassing board delay was due to his lack of familiarity with the site used to upload the results. However, he just so happened to figure it all out a mere 120 seconds after the deadline. Does anyone really believe that if the vote count would have increased the lead for Democrat candidates, those results would have been posted late? If you do, I have some swamp land to sell you...in Florida.

The inability to use the electronic recount meant that the state had to do a manual recount—that's right, people sitting in a room counting every single vote by hand with the goal of getting through every ballot within twelve hours. It also meant that individuals had some discretion as to which ballots to count and which ballots to discard. This is the complete antithesis of a fair, open and transparent system. And sadly, it has been the norm rather than the exception in Florida for decades. No one seems to be concerned with fixing this mess that wreaks havoc on elections.

It is deeply concerning that, days after the election ended, Snipes was still producing ballots that needed to be counted. If the country would launch multiple federal and congressional investigations into Russian meddling because of Facebook ads that, one, almost no one saw, and two, the bulk of which were run *after* the election, why should there not be federal investigations for *actual* election interference when an election supervisor magically produces thousands of ballots favoring one political party several days after the election and includes them in the final vote tally?

Nevertheless, Snipes still had the support of the Democratic party, including Florida Congresswoman Debbie Wasserman Schultz. This should not come as a surprise since Snipes illegally destroyed[20] ballots in a Democratic primary that helped Debbie Wasserman Schultz win her congressional race in 2016.

In the 2014 election, Snipes came under fire for creating[21] a "phantom district" to allow people to be able to use a local UPS post office box as their home address. This was meant to illegally add 2,000 votes to that election total.

She has a sordid history of breaking election law, going all the way back to the 2003 when she mixed rejected ballots with valid ballots right before a possible recount. In 2004, Snipes "lost" 58,000 absentee ballots, which would have aided[22] the campaign of Republican John Kerry. In fact, the *Daily Caller* provided[23] a list of twelve times when news stories called out Snipes for being "possibly criminal":

1. Illegally destroying ballots[24] (Sun Sentinel, May 14, 2018)

2. Absentee ballots that never arrived[25] (Miami Herald, November 6, 2018)

3. Fellow Democrats accused her precinct of individual and systemic breakdowns that made it difficult for voters to cast regular ballots[26] (Miami Herald, November 4, 2014)

4. Posted election results half an hour before polls closed – a very clear violation of election law[27]. (Miami Herald, November 2, 2018)

5. Sued for leaving amendments off of ballots[28] (Miami Herald, October 20, 2016)

6. Claiming to not have the money to notify voters when their absentee ballot expired[29] (Sun Sentinel, November 8, 2018)

7. Having official staffers campaign on official time[30] (Broward Beat, July 20, 2016)

8. Problems printing mail ballots[31] (Miami Herald, November 2, 2018)

9. Accusations of ballot stuffing[32] (Heritage, August 1, 2017)

10. Voters receiving ballots with duplicate pages[33] (Miami Herald, November 2, 2018)

11. Slow results and piles of ballots that cropped up way after Election Day[34] (The Capitolist, November 8, 2018)

12. Opening ballots in private, breaking Florida law[35] (Politico, August 13, 2018)

Despite this nearly two-decade run of election meddling, in 2018 she still presided over elections that held significance in determining the outcome of national races. It's absolutely mind-boggling that she still had a job.

When Republicans bring up the subject of election fraud—especially in Broward County—news organizations gaslight the public and pretend that such allegations have no merit. Such is the case with CBS, which commented on the 2018 midterms, actually publishing[36] the words "Republicans have not cited any evidence to back up their accusations" despite the fact that elections supervisors in the state had already been found guilty of election fraud—repeatedly.

On November 9, 2018, a state judge sided[37] with Florida Governor Rick Scott, "ordering that Republicans be granted 'immediate' access to requested information about ballots in Broward County."

Fox News reported[38]:

> *"In their lawsuit against Broward, Scott—the Republican gubernatorial incumbent narrowly leading in the state's race for a U.S. Senate seat—and the National Republican Senatorial Committee (NRSC) allege that officials there are hiding critical information about the number of votes cast and counted.*

> *"In an emergency court hearing on Friday afternoon, state Judge Carol-Lisa Phillips ruled there has 'been a violation of the Florida constitution,' as well as the state's*

public records act, by not turning over requested records.

"Phillips ordered Broward County Supervisor of Elections Brenda Snipes to allow for the 'immediate inspection' and 'photocopying' of the requested records no later than 7 p.m. Friday."

Adding to the mountain of evidence that Democrats interfered in the 2018 midterm elections are federal investigations into documents that were altered by the Florida Democratic party in four separate counties, including Broward. Democrats produced tens of thousands of ballots after the election, many of which that had signatures that didn't match the signature the election office had on file.

"Cure affidavits" are documents mailed to voters that are intended to fix irregularities. Although those documents were due back by 5pm the day *before* the election, the affidavits that were returned showed that someone altered the document to show a due date of two days *after* the election. To make matters worse, there is an audio recording of a Florida Democratic Party operative instructing a voter to send in the information *after* the election.

Politico reported[39]:

"The Florida Department of State last week asked federal prosecutors to investigate dates that were changed on official state election documents, the first voting "irregularities" it has flagged in the wake of the 2018 elections.

"The concerns, which the department says can be tied to the Florida Democratic Party, center around date changes on forms used to fix vote-by-mail ballots sent with incorrect or missing information. Known as "cure affidavits," those documents used to fix mail ballots were due no later than 5 p.m. on Nov. 5—the day before the election. But affidavits released on Tuesday by the DOS show that documents from four different counties said the ballots could be returned by 5 p.m. on Thursday, which is not accurate.

"Audio of a Florida Democratic Party caller leaving a voicemail message asking a Palm Beach County voter to fix their vote by mail ballot after Election Day, which is not allowed, was also sent to POLITICO separately. It was not part of the information turned over to federal prosecutors."

"Florida law requires that the voter signatures on mail ballots match the signature of the voter, but Dem lawyers are asking a judge to throw that law out & force Florida to count ballots with signatures that don't match the voter signature on file," Senator Marco Rubio (R-Fla.) explained[40].

The 2018 midterm election cycle confirmed that the issues that had occurred in the past in the state of Florida had not been corrected. Officials were allowed to act with impunity in their trampling on the rights of voters and in their complete disregard for state law.

It's a bright, shining beacon of corruption.

GEORGIA

The state of Georgia had its own share of controversy after the midterms. But, unlike Florida, the problems were not centered on chain-of-custody issues and votes materializing out of nowhere. They instead had to do with a phrase uttered ad nauseam in today's news cycle: voter suppression (a subject which I cheerfully dedicate an entire chapter to later).

Democratic candidate Stacey Abrams was running for governor against Republican Brian Kemp, who declared himself the winner shortly after election night after winning by a margin of more than 60,000 votes[41]. The Atlantic reported[42], "The Abrams campaign said that Abrams was about 15,000 votes behind the threshold for a runoff, with about that many outstanding mail-in ballots left to be counted. If Abrams's team can't push Kemp's vote share below 50 percent with the late returns—which would trigger a runoff election—they hope to thin the margin to the 1 percent they need to call for a recount." Ultimately, there were not enough votes to hand Abrams the win, and Kemp was certified[43] as the winner just over a week after the election.

However, it was within just days after the election that allegations of cheating emerged. Abrams accused Kemp of using his position as secretary of state to unnecessarily purge voter rolls, which forced people to have to use provisional ballots, which could then be dismissed and not counted, despite the fact that his actions were 100 percent lawful.

On November 8, *The Republic* reported[44]:

"Provisional ballots are similar to regular ballots, but they are kept separate and not counted unless the voter's eligibility is confirmed.

"The process for issuing them and determining which ones are eligible is left to state and local election officials. In Georgia, for instance, if a voter forgets a photo ID, he or she will receive a provisional ballot. In these cases, the voter must present their identification at their local election office within a few business days to have their vote count.

"If a voter's name does not appear on the list of registered voters in a precinct, he or she will also receive a provisional ballot. Later, election officials will determine if that voter was eligible to vote but voted in the wrong precinct. In that case, only the votes in races he or she was eligible to vote in will be counted.

"Federal law requires election officials to provide a way for voters to check on their provisional ballot, typically by using a toll-free phone number or a website. If a provisional ballot was not counted, a reason should be provided."

Many people in the state complained that they were not able to register to vote in time and were forced into a provisional ballot.

Georgia civil rights group Common Cause actually sued and told[45] a U.S. district judge, without a shred of evidence, that they thought the voter rolls were purged by a hacker.

One Georgia voter, Atlanta filmmaker Rahiem Shabazz, said he was driven away from the ballot box. "I want to vote for Stacey Abrams, but I won't be able to vote in the November 6 election," Shabazz told[46] a writer for *Oped News*. He was apparently one of 340,134 voters who had their names legally purged from voter rolls in 2017. So, when he went to a polling station and found out that he was no longer on the state's voting rolls, he was issued a provisional ballot. The piece by *Oped News* stated, "Shabazz, like hundreds of thousands of others, had no idea he'd been flushed from the rolls, and assumed he was still registered. Kemp sent out no notice to voters after cancelling their registrations." It continued, "He did attempt to re-register for the election, but Kemp's office informed him it would take at least three weeks to verify his registration information. Conveniently for Kemp, that would be a week past Election Day."

"Conveniently for Kemp"? Right on the state's election website[47] it clearly shows registration deadlines that must be met in order to have one's registration be processed and active for an upcoming election. Further, the processing time needed in order for a registration to be live by the 2018 midterms? Three weeks.

To verify, I actually called the Georgia secretary of state's office and spoke with someone in the elections division. I explained the situation involving Mr. Shabazz and asked about the purged voter rolls. Specifically, I mentioned that they have an online registration system that can be accessed from any device that has an internet browser and asked, "If Mr. Shabazz had simply confirmed his registration prior to the cutoff, would he have had any trouble voting?" The answer: no.

In this case, like many others, allegations of voter suppression and racism because of purged voter rolls have nothing to do with malicious actions and everything to do with a lack of personal responsibility of a potential voter who didn't bother to register on time or confirm his or her registration. Most adults know that congressional elections are held every two years, senatorial elections every six years and presidential elections every four years. So, every two years, you will submit a ballot for some type of election. Common sense would suggest that if you are passionate enough not only to vote but to complain afterward about a perceived injustice, you should be just as passionate about making sure you take the proper steps to ensure you are able to submit a ballot.

Many of the people of Georgia don't see it that way, including some officials. What we saw was the demonization of political opposition and the disparaging of the process itself. *The New Yorker* went so far[48] as to say Kemp was intentionally trying to "keep people of color from voting" in his state, despite the fact that many of the people whose provisional and mail-in ballots were rejected have justifiable reasons for their denial.

Yet, as WSB-TV in Atlanta reported[49], the Abrams campaign filed a lawsuit the Sunday after the election to:

- count more provisional ballots, including those belonging to voters who voted in the wrong county
- stop counties from rejecting ballots for what they say are arbitrary reasons, and make all counties apply the law the same way
- delay the counties from certifying their votes for twenty-four hours

These types of delay tactics amount to obstruction considering the fact that the number of outstanding ballots wouldn't be enough to hand Abrams a win. Furthermore, counting votes that were improperly cast, such as the ones cast in the wrong county, is basically asking to legitimize fraud. In addition to conveying the policy positions of their candidates, campaigns should provide specific information to potential voters on registration, polling locations and information they will need on the day of the election. Counting ballots cast by ineligible voters is neither a national crisis nor a basis of voter suppression, because the Abrams campaign failed to take these basic steps.

As of the Tuesday after the election, *Politically Georgia* reported[50] that "Kemp [led] Abrams by about 58,000 votes, but she needs to net a smaller number—roughly 21,000 votes—to force a Dec. 4 runoff against the Republican. Georgia law requires a runoff if no candidate gets a majority of the vote." However, they also wrote "Abrams' campaign is zeroing in on provisional ballots cast by voters whose information often could not be immediately verified at polling places. State records indicate roughly 21,000 of those ballots were cast statewide, but Abrams' campaign said its own review shows about 5,000 more."

The votes never came. And, as of August 2019, Abrams continued her denial tour, appearing on *CBS News* as the epitome of a pugnacious politician, still refusing to concede an election she clearly and equitably lost and embarrassing herself by desperately clinging to the illusion that she got stomped in the election because of a con. When asked why she didn't concede, she said[51], "Because concession means to say that the process was fair...I am complicit if I say that that system is fair." GOP Chairwoman Ronna McDaniel responded, writing on Twitter, "If Stacey Abrams actually cared about the integrity of elections, she'd concede the Georgia governor's race that she lost by 55,000 votes. Instead, she's on national TV today still thinking she won. Completely ridiculous.[52]"

But, this was an idea that started fairly early on. Despite Kemp having a lead of nearly 60,000 votes, Sherrod Brown (D-OH) told[53] left-wing advocacy group National Action Network a week after the election that if Abrams didn't win, it was because Republicans stole the election. They floated the ideas of suppression and racism right out of the gate.

Shortly after the election, Abrams sued, alleging that purging voter rolls and shortening the days of early voting from 45 to 21 limited the ability of Georgians to cast votes. She alleged that poorer, black counties were disproportionately affected and simply couldn't afford to stay open as long as other counties, meaning that not as many voters were able to cast ballots. There's just one problem: Abrams actually co-sponsored[54] the legislation that shortened the early voting time she now claims disenfranchises Georgia voters.

In yet another stunning example of how baseless Abrams' claims of "suppression" are, it turns out that it was her, the candidate herself—an African-American, no less—who helped bring about the very policy she somehow deems racist.

Rather than accept the fact that she lost, just like Hillary Clinton did in 2016, Abrams resorts to attacking a system she helped create and claims to be a victim. Similarly, the fact is that she lost—not because the deck was stacked against her but because she was an awful candidate banking on identity politics to make up for a lack of viability as a suitable choice for the office she sought. Despite the fact that she owed[55] the IRS more than $50,000 and had racked up roughly $170,000 in credit card and unpaid student loan debt (making her an easy target to compromise), she was an extremist pretending to be a moderate, and folks saw right through the facade. She supported gun confiscation (which is incredibly ironic, given that armed members of the New Black Panther Party touted rifles[56] while supporting her candidacy), opposed religious freedom legislation (not a winning strategy in the South) and was an advocate for illegal immigration (supporting policies that redirect precious resources away from the very minority constituents she courted).

All-in-all, the voters decided, and they chose Kemp. She lost fair and square. The only substance to claims of election manipulation were from the Abrams campaign, which hoped to undo the results of a free and fair election.

ARIZONA

Arizona was a key state to watch during the 2018 midterm elections. Nationally, the battle was on for Republicans to retain control and for Democrats to win control of the United States Senate. Arizona had been considered a guaranteed red state for some time. But, Democrat Kyrsten Sinema succeeded in helping to turn The Grand Canyon State purple[57] after her win in the race for Senate. The state's other Senate seat was occupied at the time by Republican Jon Kyl, who was selected to fill the seat just months prior to the election[58], after the passing of Arizona Senator John McCain.

The Senate balance was critical to the agenda of the Trump administration for several important reasons. First, the Senate is the body that confirms judicial nominees for federal court and the U.S. Supreme Court. Part of President Trump's campaign strategy was a promise to appoint conservative judges to the courts. As of September 30, 2019, the Senate had confirmed 152 judicial nominees, which NPR described as happening at a faster "pace than the last five presidents and stocking the courts with lifetime appointees who could have profound consequences for civil rights, the environment and government regulations.[59]" Judicial appointments are legacy items that have a much longer-lasting effect on the nation than any other policies that an administration implements. Second, the Senate is the body that holds trial, should the U.S. House of Representatives decide to impeach the president—a goal Democrats have had since before President Trump was sworn into office[60]. Even if a president is impeached by the House, they cannot be convicted and removed from office unless a two-thirds majority of the Senate votes to remove them. Therefore, electing as many conservative senators as possible was an imperative for Republicans.

Then-candidate Sinema was a very likeable, "safe" choice for Democrats and moderates, but the last time a U.S. Senate seat for Arizona was won by a Democrat was in 1988[61]. So, there wasn't a strong sense of concern over her squaring off against military veteran Martha McSally (R-Ariz.). Additionally, there were other local races that were widely watched.

So, what happened?

"On the evening of Tuesday, November 6, 2018 Arizona voters went to bed believing that Republicans had won all three close statewide races: U.S. Senate, Secretary of State, and Superintendent of Education. The highly-respected Associated Press declared victory for Republican Steve Gaynor at 10:20 pm and assured Gaynor that it almost never miscalled a race." This is the opening paragraph of a post-election report written by attorney Stephen Richer. He completed a report for the Arizona Republican Party to audit the 2018 midterm election after anomalies arose that called the results of the state's elections into question. Interviewees for the report included Elected representatives of the Arizona state legislature, Former Maricopa County Recorder Helen Purcell, officials from the Maricopa County Board of Supervisors, officials in the office of the Arizona Secretary of State, County Recorders from counties other than Maricopa, election law attorneys, Arizona voters, campaign staff and election workers.

The report continued, "But the Associated Press was somehow wrong. Not only did Gaynor's election night lead evaporate in the following days, but so too did the leads of Republicans Martha McSally and Frank Riggs. Within a week, McSally's election night lead of nearly 15,000 votes turned into a deficit of 55,900 votes; Gaynor went from a lead of over 40,000 votes to trailing by 20,252 votes; and Riggs's apparent victory by a margin of approximately 7,000 votes turned into a loss by 71,676 votes."

It's incredible to many that in yet another state during the midterm elections, Republican candidates held a lead at the time the polls closed, only to have those leads eviscerated during the tabulation process.

The *Washington Free Beacon* reported[62], "After Election Day, about 650,000 votes were not yet tallied in counties across Arizona, but the lion's share of those outstanding ballots resided in Maricopa County, the fourth-largest county[63] in the country."

As *Vox* noted[64], "Unlike some other states, Arizona requires voters to have ballots physically in by [Election Day] and doesn't count ones that are simply postmarked by that time." So, unlike in Florida, in Arizona it isn't illegal to continue counting votes beyond election night. Roughly 75 percent of Arizona's ballots are mail-in[65], which means that the signatures have to be authenticated. And in 2018, that meant that a lot of time was needed before the final results were in.

But, many were concerned that actions undertaken by state officials were done so in order to manipulate the outcome of the election. Specifically, Maricopa County Recorder Adrian Fontes came under fire after some alleged that his office made decisions in the final days of the election that were intended to damage Republicans. Richer's report would dig into these allegations as well as other items.

The report[66] focused on four key questions: (1) the Office's decision to open special emergency voting centers, (2) the Office's decision to rehabilitate ballots following election night, (3) allegations of partisan behavior by County Recorder Adrian Fontes, and (4) particularized allegations of voter fraud or irregularities in Maricopa County.

Emergency Voting Centers

County Recorder Adrian Fontes opened five emergency voting locations on the weekend before the midterm elections: Avondale City Hall, Indian Bend Wash Visitor Center, MCTEC - Elections Department, Mesa Recorder's Office and Tolleson Park & Recreation Center. Arizona has a history of using emergency voting centers, but historically with limited conditions. Arizona law ARS § 16-549(D) addresses emergency voting and defines "emergency" as "any unforeseen circumstances that would prevent the elector from voting at the polls.[67]" It also states that a signed statement under penalty of perjury is required for the person experiencing the emergency that would prevent them from voting on election day[68].

The report notes that Fontes departed from past precedent and publicized the five locations on the Recorder's social media feed, his personal social media feed and through official media channels. His predecessor, Helen Purcell, limited emergency voting to the Recorder's Office and, in the spirit of the intent of the law, it was not widely announced as simply another regular voting option. Richer's report also states that many "questioned the motivation behind Recorder Fontes's decision to expand the number of emergency voting locations and to advertise their availability," citing his previous support for two Arizona House Bills that sought to expand early voting but failed to pass. "With this as a backdrop, it seems plausible that Recorder Fontes expanded emergency voting to partially accomplish what the Arizona legislature considered but refused to authorize: expanding early voting to the Saturday, Sunday, and Monday before the Tuesday election," the report says. "Such a 'back door' to a legislative proposal would almost certainly violate the intent of emergency voting as defined in the Arizona code and in the Elections Procedure Manual."

Further complicating defense of these early voting practices is analysis of the political makeup of the only locations[69] chosen for this expanded voting effort.

- In Avondale City Hall, Democrats make up 42 percent of the electorate, compared to 16 percent Republicans.
- In the Indian Bend Wash precinct, there are 32 percent registered Democrats and 31 percent registered Republicans.
- MCTEC Elections Department precinct boasts 49 percent registered Democrats to only 13 percent registered Republicans.
- The Mesa Recorder's Office precinct shows 36 percent registered Democrats and only 21 percent Republicans.
- The Tolleson precinct has 54 percent registered Democrats and only 11 percent registered Republicans.

Many questioned why these five locations were selected. Any reasonable person could look at this information and reach the conclusion that Fontes—who is a registered Democrat—selected these five areas for extra days of voting, in whole or in part because they are areas largely dominated by Democrats and would likely increase the vote count for his party of choice. The optics here are horrible.

Despite the fact that margins of victory for the races of U.S. Senate, Superintendent and Secretary of State were greater than the number of votes reportedly cast at the emergency voting centers, questions remained and the Recorder's office was unresponsive when pressed for answers.

Ballot Rehabilitation

In Arizona, mail-in ballots needed to be postmarked by October 31 in order to be counted in the midterm elections. Any person who missed the deadline "could drop off their mail-in ballots at the in-person voting locations on Election Day, so long as those ballots were received by 7:00 p.m. on Election Day," the report said. The signature on the envelope that contains the ballot is compared to the voter's signature that is on file to verify the voter's identity, and when the signature doesn't match, there is an attempt by the Recorder's Office to cure or "rehabilitate" the ballot by contacting the voter directly.

The report stated:

> *"Prior to Recorder Fontes's time in office, Maricopa County stopped the curing/rehabilitation process at 7:00 pm on Election Night. This had the potential effect of excluding some late early ballots from being counted because if those ballots had mismatched signatures, the Recorder's Office might not have had enough time to cure the ballot received on Election Day prior to 7:00 pm that same day.*

According to Recorder Purcell, early voting is intended to in fact be early; voters have multiple weeks prior to the election to mail in their ballots. If voters choose to wait until Election Day to drop off the 'early ballot' then the burden is on them to make sure their signature matches the signature on file.

"Recorder Fontes departed from Recorder Purcell's tradition and instead chose to continue rehabilitating ballots after Election Day. This prompted a lawsuit from the Arizona Republican Party. The Republican Party claimed that '[p]rinciples of equal protection cannot abide the County Recorder Defendants' fashioning of ad hoc deadlines and variegated procedures for the disposition of facially deficient early ballots.' In other words, the Republican Party objected that votes continued to be cured in some counties -- such as Maricopa County -- while that process ended at 7:00pm on Election Day in other counties. In doing so, the Party argued, the voting system treated votes unequally."

"County Recorders are provided with limited direction regarding the curing of ballots under Section 16-550(A) of the Arizona Code and the 2014 Elections Procedures Manual. Page 166 of the Elections Procedures Manual states that 'the County Recorder, if time permits, may attempt to contact the voter to ascertain whether the voter actually voted the early ballot and any reasons why the signatures may not match.' The language 'if time permits'

*is vague and does not clearly mark a definite stop time for
the curing process."*

Yet, although the decision to continue counting ballots after
the 7:00pm deadline was a sign to some that improper activities were taking place, as the report itself notes, they "did
not violate any statutory provision of the 2014 Election
Procedures Manual."

Partisanship of Recorder Fontes

There were many allegations that Fontes was an extremely partisan figure who used his position to benefit his
preferred candidates. He certainly didn't help paint himself
as a mature, dispassionate public official operating in good
faith in the best interests of the community when he wrote
on Twitter, "Go F- yourself...by the way is your Mom also
running your campaign? She seems to solve all of your other problems" to one candidate, or when he wrote "Bring it"
in response to a lawsuit that was filed by the Arizona GOP
after the midterms.

Richer's report notes that Fontes was accused of:

1. Coordinating with the Sinema campaign "by pri-
    vately disclosing the timing and location of the
    emergency voting centers without offering the same
    information to Republican Martha McSally's cam-
    paign,"

2. Sending an "instructive and helpful private text messages to attorney Roopali Desai and/or other members of the law firm Coppersmith Brockelman PLC, counsel for the Arizona Democratic Party, regarding the fact that they would need to sue his office to obtain certain information regarding voter records, but that Recorder Fontes did not provide the same information to the attorneys representing the Martha McSally campaign or the Arizona Republican Party;"

3. Helping "place people with the campaign firm Zero Week Solutions, which assisted the Arizona Democratic Party."

In addition, Richer's report references an instance of "disparate treatment of Republican County Supervisor Steve Chucri and Democrat County Supervisor Steve Gallardo in the context of the emergency voting centers," stating:

"As previously noted, Democrat Gallardo purportedly requested that Recorder Fontes open an emergency voting center in Tolleson so as to better assist the voters in Gallardo's district. Recorder Fontes complied and worked with Supervisor Gallardo to expand emergency voting. By contrast, Republican Supervisor Chucri said he was not consulted about the locations of the emergency voting centers, and he was not even informed of the expansion of the emergency voting centers prior to their public announcement. Additionally, in an email to Recorder Fontes dated

Monday, November 5 (the day before Election Day), Supervisor Chucri told Recorder Fontes that '[d]ue to recent inquiries, I am formally asking you to place aside all ballots cast at emergency voting sites after early voting ended on Friday, November 2, 2018, until your legal authority to open emergency sites has been clarified.' Chucri claims that he received no response from Recorder Fontes on this topic. This Review has sought an interview with Recorder Fontes regarding this interplay, but Recorder Fontes has not responded. As it stands, this juxtaposition of treatment between Democrat Supervisor Gallardo and Republican Supervisor Chucri on the topic of emergency voting centers would, again, allow an observer to plausibly suspect that Recorder Fontes is not a neutral arbiter of the voting process."

Aside from Richer's report regarding possible coordination with the Sinema campaign, people have stated openly that at the time the emergency voting centers were announced, door hangers for Sinema were already made and placed on voters' doors at their homes. It would be impossible for this to have occurred unless the campaign had already been made aware of the early voting situation. Additionally, the door hangers are reported to have stated that no identification was required for early voting.

And although there is a general sentiment that Fontes is a corrupt figure, no one seemed able to corroborate any of the other allegations with facts. They can't be ruled out, however, since the Recorder's Office has declined to turn over documents that were requested to clear up this issue. But, in America, we don't operate on the presumption of guilt. And, as an attorney, surely Fontes knows this.

Fraud and Voting Irregularities

Richer's report does note some documented instances of alleged fraud that occurred in Arizona during the 2018 midterms. As it turns out, there were reportedly ballots sent out that "had been pre-marked to select Democrat candidate Kyrsten Sinema for the office of United States Senator and Democrat candidate Greg Stanton for the office of United States Representative for the Ninth District of Arizona."

According to a signed declaration, a voter who experienced this said, "The markings were not stray lines or blots; the ballot had been printed or otherwise prepared in advance with Sinema's and Stanton's names clearly and unmistakably pre-selected.

"When I pointed out the irregularity to a poll worker who was identified only by the name of 'Chris,' a man who had been behind me in line to vote stated that his ballot also contained pre-marked selections for Sinema and Stanton."

The declaration continued, "'Chris' hurriedly took the pre-marked ballots from me and the other voter and handed us replacement ballots. I was unable to observe what 'Chris' did with the pre-marked ballots. Neither 'Chris' nor any other polling place worker offered any explanation for why the other voter and I had been given ballots already pre-marked with votes cast for Sinema and Stanton."

There were also multiple reports of voters who were properly registered who were turned away from the polls and forced to vote with a provisional ballot. One voter filed a complaint that a polling location on 39th Avenue had a sign up that said "God is Love, Trump is Hate," an act that may have constituted electioneering, which is a class 2 misdemeanor in Arizona[70]. There were also reports of outages that prevented people from casting ballots.

I spoke with an Arizona political figure, who asked not to be identified, who stated that in the 2018 election cycle, there were multiple progressive groups that handled voter registration as well as Democrats, who discussed on a conference call that they were engaging in ballot harvesting in Arizona. Ballot harvesting in the state is illegal. However, since the ballots are simply dropped off, there would have been no way to enforce the law and catch anyone engaging in this practice. Considering the reports of large-scale absentee ballot fraud (more on this later), it's plausible that this handed a significant number of votes to Democratic candidates in 2018.

Takeaways

In its handling of the 2018 midterm elections, election officials in Arizona clearly played favorites by opening early voting centers only in majority Democrat-held areas. During the ballot curing process, Maricopa County officials broke with past precedent to stop counting early ballots at 7:00pm and continued for days—while other counties did not—which disenfranchised rural voters who were more likely to support a Republican. Overall, there were many instances of irregularities that took place. Jim Bognet, CEO of then-candidate McSally's campaign, wrote on Twitter[71], "There are and continue to be multiple instances of electoral irregularities in Arizona, including extreme incompetence and possible purposeful misconduct in Maricopa County. The Campaign worked closely with the NRSC and RNC to investigate and address any alleged misconduct that voters discovered. While the margin grew to a point where these issues seemed unlikely to tip the scale in our race, there are still undecided races where these occurrences could tip the balance. These issues MUST be addressed." The problem is that you need proof to turn irregularities into violations of the law. (Yes, ballot harvesting is illegal, but it was not investigated after it was reported.)

Fontes' office refused to provide any paper trail about the activities that took place and refused interviews to provide more transparency to a public hungry for more information. And, although there were myriad allegations of election manipulation levied against him and his office, little could actually be corroborated.

CHAPTER 3

Dead Voters & Ghost Voters

"Dead people generally vote for Democrats rather than Republicans."

—*Rudy Giuliani, Former New York City mayor*

Data from the U.S. Census Bureau show[1] that America has millions more registered voters than it does living voters. These types of voters are often referred to as ghost voters. Deroy Murdock of *National Review* took a deep dive into the issue of ghost voters and the potential impact they could have on U.S. elections. Murdock says[2], "Some 3.5 million more people are registered to vote in the U.S. than are alive among America's adult citizens. Such staggering inaccuracy is an engraved invitation to voter fraud."

Murdock said that at least 462 counties exhibit this

ghost voter problem, citing areas like Washington state's Clark County, which has a 154 percent voter registration rate and Georgia's Fulton County, which has a 108 percent registration rate.

California is especially troubling, given its size. California actually has eleven separate counties with more registered voters than eligible voters, and ten of those counties voted[3] for Hillary Clinton in the 2016 election. The *LA Times* ran a headline in 2016 saying[4], "There are now more registered voters in California than the population of 46 states," which was characterized as a positive milestone. Keep reading, and you'll see why state officials were pleased with the data.

San Diego County's registration rate of 138 percent translates to more than 810,000 ghost voters, and Los Angeles County's 112 percent over-registrations suggests more than 700,000 ghost voters. (After updating the numbers, LA County employees reported[5] that "the total number of registered voters now stands at a number that is a whopping 144 percent of the total number of resident citizens of voting age.") So, based on the data, it is possible that just two counties in California alone could contribute more than 1.5 million illegal votes toward an election. (More on this in Chapter 4, which discusses purging voter rolls.)

Murdock reported that Judicial Watch (JW) president Tom Fitton gave a statement saying, "California's voting rolls are an absolute mess[6] that undermines the very idea of clean elections."

The inability of states like California to purge voter rolls creates a clear opportunity for election meddling. *Western Journal* posted[7] the numbers for ghost voters in several swing states:

- Colorado: 159,373
- Florida: 100,782
- Iowa: 31,077
- Michigan: 225,235
- New Hampshire: 8,211
- North Carolina: 189,721
- Virginia: 89,979

If these numbers are not concerning, it is important to keep in mind the razor-thin margins by which many elections are won in this country, including the 2016 presidential election between Hillary Clinton and then-candidate Donald Trump. Consider the following:

- Clinton only won Colorado by a margin of 136,386 votes, but the state boasts 159,373 ghost voters.
- Clinton won New Hampshire by only 2,736 votes, but the state has 8,211 ghost voters.
- President Trump won Michigan by 10,704 votes, yet that state has 225,235 ghost-voters.
- President Trump won North Carolina with a 173,315 margin, yet that state has 189,721 ghost-voters

"When you have an extremely large number of stale names

on the voter rolls in a county, it makes voter fraud much easier to commit," Secretary of State Kris Kobach[8] (R-Kan.), co-chairman of President Trump's Advisory Commission on Election Integrity, told *National Review*. "It's easier to identify a large number of names of people who have moved away or are deceased. At that point, if there is no photo-ID requirement in the state, those identities can be used to vote fraudulently."

National Review also reported that federal law requires states to maintain accurate voter rolls: "The 1993 National Voter Registration Act (a.k.a. Motor Voter) holds that "A State shall . . . systematically remove the names of ineligible voters from the official lists of eligible voters." (42 U.S. Code § 1973gg-6(c)(2)(A)). This is for purposes of ensur[ing] that accurate and current voter registration rolls are maintained." (42 USC § 1973gg(h)(4))." That said, efforts to do so are often met with considerable resistance. For instance, when Florida GOP governor Rick Scott tried to obey these laws and update the state's records, including deleting 51,308 deceased voters[9], Obama's justice department filed a federal lawsuit to stop him.

Florida "compared its voter rolls against drivers license applications, which contain citizenship information. It discovered 182,000 potential non-citizens who were registered voters." A state spokesman told Murdock that "a subsample of 2,600 of these 182,000 possible aliens yielded at least 500[10] now-naturalized citizens as well as, so far, 104 confirmed non-citizen registered voters, 56 of whom feloniously have voted." Murdock continued, "If this sample is representative, it extrapolates to 7,280 registered non-citizens, 3,920 of whom may have voted and may do so again. Given that George W. Bush won Florida and thus the White House by just 537 votes, Americans should rail against the possibility that more than *seven times* as many aliens could be poised to elect the next president of the United States."

Simply put, there is no way to guarantee honest elections with this much potential for fraud. Even international leaders have shunned[11] the U.S. voting system, saying that "there's often no way to know if one person has voted several times under different names." Ghost voting provides the perfect conduit for such fraud. The mere potential for this much abuse should sound an alarm and lead to bipartisan calls for reform. And, although there are many people pushing to ameliorate this problem, they tend to be conservatives.

Eric Eggers, research director for the Government Accountability Institute (GAI), told[12] *Breitbart News Daily* that voter fraud is a serious issue in the U.S.

"You have 248 counties in this country that have more registered voters than you have citizens of legal voting age … nearly three million people are registered to vote in more than one state," Eggers said. "Even Barack Obama's … administration said that … maybe 16 million election registrations are completely inaccurate. And in some states, this is as many as one-in-seven [registrations]." He also said that part of the strategy for delaying measures to increase election security is to level "charges of racism anytime a state wants to do anything" to combat voter fraud. Eggers, an election fraud expert, even went so far as to say that the "Democratic Party political machine is built in part on the reliance of illegal votes cast by demographics that vote reliably for Democrats." Please read that last sentence again.

For years, multiple states and counties across the country have had issues with voter rolls. In 2015, the Public Interest Legal Foundation (PILF) notified[13] 141 counties across the United States that, according to federally produced data, they have more registered voters than they have people alive, stating that they were in violation of federal law by not purging names from their voter rolls.

"Corrupted voter rolls provide the perfect environment for voter fraud," said J. Christian Adams, President and General Counsel of PILF on their website. "Close elections tainted by voter fraud turned control of the United States Senate in 2009. Too much is at stake in 2016 to allow that to happen again."

"The letters inform the target counties that it appears they are violating the NVRA because they are not properly maintaining the voter rolls," PILF said in a press release[14]. "Having more registrants than eligible citizens alive indicates that election officials have failed to properly maintain voter rolls."

Specifically, PILF noted the following states received a notice letter (number of counties indicated in parentheses): Michigan (24), Kentucky (18), Illinois (17), Indiana (11), Alabama (10), Colorado (10), Texas (9), Nebraska (7), New Mexico (5), South Dakota (5), Kansas (4), Mississippi (4),

Louisiana (3), West Virginia (3), Georgia (2), Iowa (2), Montana (2), North Carolina (2), Arizona, Missouri, New York.

In fact, nearly all states in the U.S. have issues with ghost voters. Here are a few[15] of the worst offenders, by state and over-registered voters:

California - 1,736,556
Michigan - 225,235
North Carolina - 189,721
Washington - 168,891
Indiana - 187,207
Illinois - 116,208
Georgia - 190,376
Florida - 100,782
Colorado - 159,373

These figures are concerning. No state should have more registered voters than eligible voters. If we are to meet the call of those wanting to eliminate the prospect of "election meddling," there needs to be legislation or court action that prevents the possibility of ghost votes impacting an election.

DEAD VOTERS

Similar to ghost votes, voter rolls can be exploited by using the names of people registered to vote who can't actually make it to the polls—because they're dead. If the existence of ghost voters doesn't necessitate reform, then the fact that America actually has people voting in the names of the deceased should.

David Goldstein a reporter for CBS in Los Angeles, CA, reported that in Southern California, there are hundreds of dead people who have "voted" in elections since the time of their deaths. John Cenkner was a local resident who passed away in 2003. Yet, "he somehow voted from the grave[16] in 2004, 2005, 2006, 2008 and 2010." After comparing local voting records with the Social Security Administration, Goldstein found 265 dead voters in Southern California and 215 in Los Angeles alone.

CBS also reported on Julita Abutin, who died in 2006 but somehow managed to vote in Norwalk in the 2014, 2012, 2010 and 2008 elections. Although it's impossible that she voted, the Los Angeles County Registrar confirms they have signed vote-by-mail envelopes with Abutin's name on them for the 2014 and 2012 elections.

Of the hundreds of names of dead voters, 86 were registered Republicans and 146 were Democrats. Most were still eligible to vote in the 2016 presidential primary election.

"It's very troubling because it basically dilutes the voice of the lawful voter," said Ellen Swensen[17] of True the Vote, a nationwide voter-rights group. "What it does is every single vote that's cast by a dead voter actually cancels out a vote of a lawful voter cause if they voted for one candidate and you voted let's say for another, your vote got canceled out," she said.

Just as we see with other types of fraud, the practice of using the identity of the deceased to cast an illegal ballot is happening all over the country. In 2012, Pew Research published a report[18] that showed there were more than 1.8 million dead people listed as registered voters across the U.S.

In 2016, CBS Chicago found[19] that "119 dead people had voted 229 times in Chicago in the last decade." They asked political consultant Dan Rose about the findings, who said[20], "Some of these could be accidental or just some individual who says, 'I really like such and such a candidate so I'm going to take advantage of this—vote until they stop me.'" Chicago's "Democratic Machine" has a long history of exploiting inaccurate voter rolls to cast ballots by people who are actually dead. "Electoral rolls are supposed to keep track of who is registered to vote. The rolls would be rigged so dead people's names still appeared on them, meaning others could vote for the candidate of their choice in the dead person's name," said Bob Crawford[21], a retired journalist who covered Chicago politics. "Sometimes, people working for the Machine would even go into cemeteries and take the names off of tombstones, then go back and fill out voter registration cards with the dead person's names as if they were still alive."

In Alaska, there were[22] seven ballots requested in the names of dead people for the 2018 midterm primary election. While seven potential votes may not seem like cause for concern, consider that Democrat Aaron Weaver only had a three-vote lead over Republican candidate Gabrielle LeDoux. And, although ballots for those particular requests weren't sent out, it does not necessarily mean that no fraudulent activity ever took place, as it's Alaska's policy to allow questionable ballots because they don't want to risk "disenfranchising voters." To put it another way, they would rather err on the side of potential election tampering.

In Colorado, an investigation by CBS[23] found multiple instances of dead people not only listed on voter rolls but actively voting in elections after their deaths. Sara Sosa of Colorado Springs was one such woman. Despite having passed away in 2009, ballots were cast in her name in 2010, 2011, 2012 and 2013. When asked about the findings of the investigation, El Paso County Clerk and Recorder Chuck Broerman called the findings "very serious" and described what happened as "illegal." So, there is no ambiguity about the fact that using the identity of the deceased to vote in an election is against the law. Yet, it's happening throughout the state. The report said:

> *"State voting officials say they can only delete names from voting rolls if a number of precise criteria from death databases are met: names must be spelled precisely right, dates of birth must be correct and addresses must match. They say in many cases minor errors on the voter rolls or death databases leave election officials no choice but to leave dead people registered, leading to potential fraud and mistaken votes."*

Other authentication methods should be pursued by local officials to properly identify dead voters and remove their names from voter rolls. Even in states like Colorado, it doesn't take many names to swing an election. Take, for example, the 2002 election in Colorado's 7th Congressional district—a race that was decided by just 121 votes.

In North Carolina, as of 2014, a letter to their Elections Oversight Committee showed[24] 13,416 deceased voters listed on their active voter rolls—a decline from 2012 when 30,000 dead voters[25] were on voter rolls. According to the EOC audit, at least 81 dead people have been confirmed voting from the grave. Also, in North Carolina a woman in Catawba County turned in an absentee ballot for her mother, who died days before the election. The Charlotte Observer reported[26] the mother as saying, "If anything happens to me, you have my power of attorney, and you be sure to vote for Donald Trump." The daughter, unaware that she had even committed a crime, was not prosecuted. District Attorney David Learner, chief prosecutor for Catawba said, "She made a mistake out of sheer ignorance without any intent to defraud or commit a crime. She was grieving the loss of her mother and believed that the power of attorney allowed her to cast this vote." The only time dead voting is really legal is in jurisdictions like Indiana[27] and Texas that have passed laws allowing absentee ballots to be counted from people who submitted them lawfully but passed away prior to the election day.

The state of Florida discovered[28] 53,000 dead people on its voter rolls back in 2012. In this case, Florida acted, and the names were purged[29] and the state began verifying names against the Social Security Death Index, a database that houses information for people whose deaths were reported to the Social Security Administration. J. Christian

Adams of PJ Media wrote[30], "Most states aren't using the same database that Florida is. In fact, I have heard reports that some election officials won't even remove voters even when they are presented with a death certificate. That means that voter rolls across the nation still are filled with dead voters, even if Florida is leading the way in detecting and removing them."

Adams also mentioned the case of a Portland resident named Lafayette Keaton, who, Adams wrote, "not only voted for a dead person in Oregon, he voted for his *dead son*." The Heritage Foundation's Election Fraud Cases[31] database shows that Keaton pleaded guilty to election officials and was "sentenced to three months' imprisonment, fined $5,000 and was placed in a one-year post-prison supervision program." Also, in Oregon's King County, election officials announced[32] they would prosecute three people who were alleged to have cast absentee ballots for their dead relatives.

In Wausau, Wisconsin, a 70-year-old man was charged with voter fraud for allegedly sending in absentee ballots in the name of his late mother. The woman died in January 2018, but her ballot was cast later that year for the August primary election. According to the Wausau Daily Herald, the City Clerk's office[33] "discovered he also sent an absentee ballot in his mother's name during the April race for Marathon County Board, Wausau City Council and Wausau School Board."

And back East, in New York's Nassau County, more than 6,000 dead people were registered to vote[34] back in

2013, and records showed that roughly 270 of them had cast ballots after their deaths. Despite assurances that there was no malice involved and that these were all honest mistakes, the reporting demonstrates the insecurity of our elections.

One person, one vote. That is how American elections are supposed to operate. Yet, our faith in this system has been compromised through policies that introduce the potential for fraud. However, the problem of ghost voters and dead voters has a rather easy solution: purge those names from voter rolls.

CHAPTER 4

Purging Voter Rolls

"Democracy must be something more than
two wolves and a sheep voting on what to
have for dinner."

—*James Bovard*

In order to vote in America, you must first register. This
can be done in multiple ways. A voter registration can be
completed by an individual on their own by going to their
state's secretary of state website. It can be done automatically—as in the case of states that automatically register
people to vote when they get driver's licenses—and there
can even be third party groups that facilitate voter registration. Once that has been completed, one's name is added to
the state's voter roll, a database listing all those who have
registered in the state. Pew Trusts says[1] that "voter registration lists are used to assign precincts, send sample ballots,

provide polling place information, identify and verify voters at polling places, and determine how resources, such as paper ballots and voting machines, are deployed on Election Day." Still, across the country, we often find that these master lists of voters are riddled with inaccuracies.

Given that, throughout the United States, there are counties with more registered voters on their voter rolls than they have living or eligible voters, there is clearly the potential for fraud. The two main reasons for incorrect voter rolls are that a person has died, or a person has moved from their residence to another county or another state. Without the sharing of voter information, there is no way another state or county would be able to determine exactly how many people are registered to vote in more than one location. This vulnerability in our system is able to be exploited nationwide by people who cast multiple or illegal ballots in elections. And, just like other types of election fraud, it may be difficult to catch. Again, we fortunately already have a sensible remedy for this problem: purge voter rolls.

The National Voter Registration Act[2] of 1993 requires states to remove inactive registrations from their voter rolls. Purges are therefore not uncommon. Between 2004 and 2006, 39 states and the District of Columbia purged[3] 39 million names from voter rolls. However, this issue turned highly contentious in the 2016 and 2018 elections, as Democrats accused Republicans of using voter roll purges to try and disenfranchise voters. They blamed racism (are you noticing a pattern here?) and purported that voter roll purges disproportionately impact minorities.

Despite such histrionics, what we find on the issue of purging voter rolls is similar to what's been shown elsewhere in this book: there are plenty of valid justifications for the voter roll purging policy, which render allegations of minority disenfranchisement null and void.

In 2016, CBS News reported[4] on a data analysis firm called Targetsmart, which said that Indiana's "voter database is riddled with errors." TargetSmart said it "found 837,000 voters with out-of-date addresses when compared to the United States Postal Service address database, or roughly one-in-five of all Indiana registered voters. The review found 4,556 duplicate registrations, 3,000 records without dates of birth and 31 records of registered voters who are too young to cast a ballot. More than 2,500 people on the rolls were listed over the age of 110." This means that in the state of Indiana alone, there existed the potential for thousands of double and illegal votes to be cast.

State police launched an investigation into voter fraud after a county clerk noticed irregularities in the registrations. The investigation, which involved more than two dozen officers, investigated 56 Indiana counties, and detectives did find evidence[5] of voter registration fraud. Connie Lawson, Indiana Secretary of State, said that there were potentially thousands of fraudulent registrations involved in the case.

Just ten years prior, Indiana had to settle a case with the U.S. Department of Justice (DOJ) after it was found to have hundreds of thousands of ineligible voters on its voter rolls—as many as 29,000 dead people and 290,000 duplicate voter registrations.

Shortly after the 2016 election, Indiana purged[6] more than 481,000 names from its voter rolls in an effort to reduce the possibility of malfeasance.

"When I became secretary of state, I discovered voter list maintenance was not being done statewide and many outdated voter registrations were still on the rolls," said[7] Lawson. "Updating these records will help us create a more accurate picture of voter turnout for the state, which has been reported as inaccurately low due to the large number of outdated registrations, while protecting the integrity of our elections." Despite that purge, like a game of whack-a-mole, Indiana still found itself with thousands more ineligible names popping up on its voter rolls.

Indiana state police superintendent Doug Carter said that he[8] believes "there's voter fraud and voter forgery in every state of America." This statement wasn't made by a partisan political hack; it wasn't made by an internet troll on social media; it was made by a senior member of law enforcement who conducted an investigation into this topic, who also can reasonably be assumed to be in contact with his peers in other states. But, despite demonstrable fraud, efforts to purge ineligible voters from the rolls in Indiana still met resistance.

In 2017, Indiana passed Senate Bill 442[9], which included a provision that allowed the state to purge names from its voter rolls after verifying them through a system called Crosscheck. The Interstate Crosscheck program compares names, dates of birth and social security numbers of a person in one state to those in other states to determine if someone is registered to vote in multiple states. The system was criticized[10] for allegedly not using enough data points and flagging legally registered voters as ineligible. The cardinal sin of the bill, however, was not that it required checking names in the Crosscheck system but that it allowed names to be removed immediately after being flagged, which is a violation of the NVRA.

On August 23, 2017, the Brennan Center filed a lawsuit[11] on behalf of the NAACP and League of Women Voters of Indiana on the basis that Senate Bill 442 violated the NVRA by "eliminating requirements to provide a notice and waiting period for a group of voters flagged by the Crosscheck program…" The Brennan Center also stated that "the NVRA provides that before voters can be removed because of change of residence, they must either confirm that they have moved or receive a mailed notice that they are going to be removed, fail to respond, and fail to vote in two consecutive federal elections." In other words, additional steps must be taken to try and avoid removing legitimate/legal voters from voter rolls, even if there is a hit in the Crosscheck database.

In 2018, the Supreme Court heard a case involving Indiana's neighbor, Ohio, in a similar case involving voter roll purges and the notice that must be provided after a name on a voter roll is flagged to potentially be ineligible.

Web magazine *Mother Jones* summed up that case, saying[12], "The state of Ohio sends a notice every year to voters who have not cast a ballot in the previous two-year cycle. Voters are asked to respond to the notice, update their registration online, or vote sometime in the next four years. If they do none of these things, they are removed from the rolls, ostensibly in an effort to prevent voter fraud by removing ineligible names. The issue before the court was whether this process violates the NVRA's prohibition on removing voters because of their failure to cast a ballot."

The case began with a man named Larry Harman, a software engineer, who usually only cast ballots in presidential elections. NPR reported[13]:

> *"In 2012, he didn't like the Obama-Romney choice, and so he stayed home. And when he went to vote a couple of years later, against a ballot initiative about marijuana legalization, he found he was no longer registered. He had been purged from the rolls, because he hadn't voted in two consecutive elections, nor had he sent back a postcard the state sent out to confirm that his address had not changed.*

> *"Harmon has lived at the same address for more than 16 years but doesn't ever remember receiving such a letter. So he sued the state, contending there are lots of other ways to confirm an address, including checking property records, tax forms, and drivers' licenses. 'I earned the right to vote,' said the navy veteran. 'Whether I use it or not is up to my personal discretion. They don't take away my right to buy a gun if I don't buy a gun.'*

*"The lower courts said that Ohio's voter-purge law vio-
lated the National Voter Registration Act, which says that
people may not be purged from the voter rolls because of
their failure to vote. But on Monday, the Supreme Court
said Ohio is not stripping people of the right to vote solely
because they failed to vote, but also because they didn't return the address confirmation form."*

The Court ruling re-affirmed that we do have a framework
within which legal purges of voter rolls are allowed to take
place. Ohio was acting in a good-faith effort to mitigate the
potential for wrongdoing in its elections, especially considering that there were hundreds of registered voters over the
age of 116 on its voter rolls as of 2018[14]. Mr. Harman said
that he "earned the right to vote." Aside from the fact that
his voting rights are conferred by the constitution, not his
service, the state's actions in no way rescinded that right. As
we saw with the case in Georgia, had Mr. Harman simply
taken the time to confirm his registration online, he would
have avoided this entire situation.

Purging voter rolls is a common-sense measure that
helps to eliminate the potential for double voting, so states
are well within their rights to delete ineligible names, because across multiple states, we see evidence that double
voting does occur. And while some may question the effica-
cy of the Crosscheck system, its use has yielded results.

In North Carolina, after using the Crosscheck system,
state auditors found thousands of cases of voter fraud involving people who voted in more than one state and after

their recorded deaths. "The audit showed[15] 155,692 registered North Carolina voters whose first and last names, dates of birth and last four digits of their Social Security number match those of voters registered in other states, but who most recently registered or voted elsewhere," said Guy Benson, writing for[16] Townhall.com. "A total of 35,750 voters with matching first and last names and date of birth were registered in North Carolina and another state, and voted in both states in the 2012 general election. Another 765 voters with an exact match of first and last name, date of birth and last four digits of their Social Security number were registered and voted in the 2012 general election in North Carolina and another state…"

Benson then contextualizes these startling numbers by reminding us that President Obama carried North Carolina by only 15,000 votes[17] in the 2012 election, fewer than half the number of double votes that could have been counted. To understand the cynicism of election security hawks, please consider that prior to Obama, North Carolina had not elected a Democrat for president in 32 years. Should the country simply ignore the fact that Obama's historic win could have possibly been connected to the tens of thousands of people in North Carolina who were able to vote twice for Lord knows how many years? It's worth noting that North Carolina only checked its voter rolls with 28 other states, not all 49. So, tens of thousands of other people may have also been able to cast multiple ballots in those elections as well.

"Voter fraud undeniably exists," wrote Benson. "The

extent to which it exists remains unclear, as the stunning results of North Carolina's audit demonstrate." Herein lies the problem with inaccurate voter rolls: they erode faith in the electoral system, because it's difficult to assess whether or not cheating actually occurred. It's worth noting that in 2018, North Carolina purged 576,534[18] registrations from its voter rolls, which represents a step in the right direction.

In Texas, an official was forced to resign[19] after trying to purge voter rolls before a presidential election. Hope Andrade, Texas Secretary of State, spearheaded an effort to remove dead voters from the rolls ahead of the presidential election. Her office sent out notices to roughly 80,000 people that, according to federal records, were potentially deceased. However, the list included people who were still alive. A lawsuit was filed by several living voters affected by this measure, a lawyer for whom said[20] Andrade had "exceeded her authority by pursuing a voter purge based on weak matches." A temporary restraining order was issued barring the state from cancelling the registrations of voters who didn't respond to the notice.

Of course, controversy ensued after it was alleged the mix-up was intentional and aimed at (insert eyeroll) suppressing the minority vote—a completely asinine allegation, considering Andrade was the state's first Latina secretary of state. San Antonio, TX attorney Roy Barrera said[21], "In some efforts it was legitimate, in others it was just an effort to hold down the vote—in my opinion—of minorities. I don't think she took any role in that effort, but yes, she did send letters to many, many people over the state inquiring about their qualifications."

Others also jumped into the fray and used an incident that was likely the result of basic human error to fuel accusations of racism. "The secretary of state has notified 80,000 individuals that it says are deceased," Texas Democratic Party Chairman Gilberto Hinojosa said[22]. "And so when a Hispanic is being told that he's dead, most sociologists will tell you a Hispanic is probably more prone to just accept it and walk away, say, 'Somebody made a mistake. I don't have time to bother with this.'"

NPR reported that, in Houston, the city got hundreds of calls from elderly people who received the notice, though they were very much alive. "We're required by law to maintain a clean and accurate voter registration list, and we're attempting to comply with that mandate," said Rich Parsons[23], a spokesman for the Texas secretary of state. "I will tell you that it was our hope to have done this after the March primary, but unfortunately, redistricting litigation delayed the primary and the associated deadlines." In response to so many living voters getting caught in the mix-up, the city of Houston decided to take no action to remove names from voter rolls until after that year's election.

Anomalies in voter rolls are an occurrence around the nation. In 2017, Judicial Watch sent a notice of violation letters threatening to sue[24] 11 states that had counties with more registered voters than voting-age citizens. The full list of states and counties included:

Alabama: Choctaw, Conecuh, Greene, Hale, Lowndes, Macon, Marengo, Perry, Washington, Wilcox

Florida: Clay, Flagler, Okaloosa, Osceola, Santa Rosa, St. Johns

Georgia: Bryan, Columbia, DeKalb, Fayette, Forsyth, Fulton, Lee, Marion, McIntosh, Oconee

Illinois: Alexander, Bureau, Cass, Clark, Crawford, DuPage, Franklin, Grundy, Hardin, Henderson, Jefferson, Jersey, Massac, McHenry, Mercer, Monroe, Pulaski, Rock Island, Sangamon, Scott, Union, Wabash, Washington, White

Iowa: Scott, Johnson

Kentucky: Anderson, Bath, Boone, Breathitt, Caldwell, Carlisle, Cumberland, Fulton, Gallatin, Greenup, Hancock, Henry, Jefferson, Jessamine, Kenton, Livingston, Magoffin, McCracken, Menifee, Mercer, Monroe, Oldham, Powell, Russell, Scott, Spencer, Trigg, Trimble, Wolfe, Woodford

Maryland: Montgomery

New Jersey: Essex, Somerset

New York: Nassau

North Carolina: Buncombe, Camden, Chatham, Cherokee, Clay, Dare, Durham, Guilford, Madison, Mecklenburg, New Hanover, Orange, Union, Watauga, Yancey

Tennessee: Williamson

"Dirty election rolls can mean dirty elections," said Judicial Watch President Tom Fitton[25] in a press release. "These 11 states face possible Judicial Watch lawsuits unless they follow the law and take reasonable steps to clean up their voting rolls of dead, moved, and non-citizen voters." Obviously, actions by JW to force compliance with the NVRA were met with resistance, including by the state of Maryland, which actually accused the watchdog group of having ties to Russian agents. JW called the allegation[26] "baseless" and retaliation "against an organization and its supporters because of their conservative political views, a violation of the First Amendment." With such inaccurate voter rolls, the states were in violation of the NVRA and exposed their elections to the potential for fraud.

The actions of JW yielded results. In 2018, a federal court judge issued a consent decree forcing Kentucky[27] "to remove the names of ineligible voters no longer in residence from its official voter registration lists." JW said that the plan also had to include:

- *Procedures for a general program of list maintenance*
- *Sources of information used regularly*
- *Procedures for sending a non-forwardable canvass mailing*
- *Procedures for using the data that is successfully matched to the statewide voter registration list*
- *Timing of notices and updates*
- *List of registrants to whom notices have been sent.*
- *Procedures for removing from the statewide voter registration list any registrant who is mailed a notice*
- *A description of databases to be used in list maintenance activities and a plan to consult with relevant database managers, assess the quality of data to be used in list maintenance activities, and develop sound and reliable matching criteria*

- *Procedures for maintaining and making available for inspection and copying the records concerning implementation of the general program activities*
- *A detailed description of any role that local election officials may play in list maintenance activities.*
- *Public outreach*

In an even bigger win, Judicial Watch won its lawsuit against California, which in 2019 was forced to remove 1.5 million inactive voters from its voter rolls. "The new settlement agreement, filed today with U.S. District Court Judge Manuel L. Real, requires all of the 1.5 million potentially ineligible registrants to be notified and asked to respond," Judicial Watch reported. "If there is no response, those names are to be removed as required by the NVRA."

Business & Politics reported[28], "California Secretary of State Padilla also agrees to update the State's online NVRA manual to make clear that ineligible names must be removed and to notify each California county that they are obligated to do this. This should lead to cleaner voter rolls statewide."

Lawsuits to force compliance with the NVRA are neither new, nor solely filed by conservative watchdog organizations. The U.S. Department of Justice said[29] that right after the NVRA became effective "several states failed to take the steps necessary to comply with the law," forcing the DOJ to file lawsuits. The first round of states included California, Illinois, Michigan, Mississippi, Pennsylvania,

New York, South Carolina, Vermont and Virginia. Ultimately, the states were ordered to comply.

The writing has been on the wall for some time regarding America's abhorrent voter rolls. Way back in 2012, Pew Trusts released a report on the need to upgrade the country's voter registration system, citing the extent of a problem by saying that[30] "approximately 24 million—one of every eight—voter registrations in the United States are no longer valid or are significantly inaccurate, more than 1.8 million deceased individuals are listed as voters" and "approximately 2.75 million people have registrations in more than one state."

The study also determined that roughly 24 million voter registration records were found to be inaccurate or no longer valid. Clearly, it is a problem that persisted far after the 2012 election cycle.

But, even as accurate as a state's voter rolls may be, practices such as same-day registration can circumvent the authentication process. For example, in 2016 in the state of Wisconsin, more than 368,000 people registered to vote on election day. With same-day registrations, voters are allowed to cast ballots, then the local jurisdiction sends postcards after the election to verify that the information provided to register is valid and accurate.

Chris Rochester, from the MacIver Institute, wrote[31], "When the state sent postcards to their addresses to verify their residency after the election, 10,461 came back as undeliverable. Local officials claim they were able to reconcile all but 3,871 of them. That means, officially, 3,871 voters in the 2016 election cannot be verified and potentially voted illegally. In Milwaukee County alone 44,797 people registered to vote on election day and 2,563 postcards bounced back to election officials. Unofficially, there could be as many as 10,461 cases of voter fraud from the 2016 election due to election day registrations (EDR) alone."

State Elections Commission spokesman Reid Magney said[32], "If the postcard comes back to the municipal clerk as undeliverable, the clerk shall remove the voter from the eligible list and provide the voter's name to the district attorney's office." With that in mind, it's rather concerning that only 954 people were referred to the district attorney for investigation and potential prosecution.

In 2019, Arizona state lawmakers were floating a bill that would purge names from the mail-in ballot list if they have not voted[33] "in either the primary or general election for two consecutive election cycles for federal, statewide or legislative office." Estimates show that had such a system been in place for the 2016 and 2018 elections, roughly 200,000 names would have been purged from the rolls. And, not to anyone's surprise, as local news outlet *Arizona Central* reported, the bill "is opposed by progressive and voter-advocacy groups, who fear it would suppress voter turnout among young people and people of color," despite there being absolutely no evidence that it would. And, after all of the anomalies in the 2018 midterms in Arizona, seeing legislation emerge to try and prevent voter fraud should be expected.

In 2018, the Brennan Center released a report[34] on voter purges. The report focuses largely on errors across the country when states have purged their rolls over the years. There are some instances where states engaged in illegal purges—Florida, New York, North Carolina and Virginia. But, it falls short in failing to address the millions of cases of *legitimate* purges that may have been successful in preventing fraudulent ballots from being cast. One might easily suspect the motive for the report's myopia upon reading their list of solutions, which includes passing automatic voter registration—a measure that registers untold numbers of people who are ineligible to vote.

Over the years, millions of names have been purged from voter rolls across the country. The Brennan Center report cites nearly 16 million voters removed between 2014 and 2016 alone. But, even considering those figures, "95 percent of American adults said they either had never, or hardly ever, had an issue with their voter registration before," according to a NPR/Marist College poll[35].

Despite all of the hysteria surrounding this topic (such as the Brennan Center saying[36] purges are a "growing threat to the right to vote"), purging voter rolls remains an effective and necessary measure to help eliminate the potential for election fraud.

CHAPTER 5

Ballot Harvesting

"The vote is a trust more delicate than any other, for it involves not just the interests of the voter, but his life, honor and future as well."

—*Jose Marti*

"'Ballot Harvesting' Helped Flip Seven U.S. House Races in California After Election Day" is a headline that ran in *The Epoch Times* on December 4, 2018, shortly after the midterm elections. If you are someone who has expressed concern over "election interference," "the sanctity of our vote," "election meddling," "foreign interference in our elections," or any other now-cliché term used to describe an outside actor potentially tampering with a vote, you should be appalled that that headline ever ran.

In America, it should be impossible to "flip" an election weeks after the polls have closed. Yet in California, Republicans saw massive numbers of votes completely wiped out after the election was over because of a practice that is illegal in much of the country—one that is banned because the potential for fraud is so incredibly high that fair-minded people oppose it.

Ballot harvesting is the practice where voters fill out a mail-in ballot or absentee ballot rather than go to the polls, and a campaign or third-party entity sends a representative to pick that ballot up. While it may add a layer of convenience for the person unable (or unwilling) to cast a ballot in person, it also adds immense potential for fraud. Since individual states regulate their own election practices, there is no national standard establishing the legality of or specific rules for ballot harvesting. In some states, it is illegal. In some states, the practice has been greatly expanded. California is one of the states that has clearly benefited from this controversial practice.

In all, seven Republican candidates in California ended up losing their races after absentee ballots were counted, despite the fact that they were winning on election night.

The Epoch Times quoted[1] then-Speaker of the House Paul Ryan (R-Wis.), who was flabbergasted at the surprising number of Republican losses, saying they "defied logic." Shortly after the election, Ryan told the *Washington Post*[2], "We had a lot of wins that night, and three weeks later, we lost basically every contested California race. This election system they have, I can't begin to understand what ballot harvesting is."

Well, when one considers that the state's ballot harvesting operations changed the results in favor of only Democrats, it's fairly easy to see what it is. Not a single Republican candidate benefited from California's ballot harvesting. Just like we saw with ballots mysteriously appearing in Florida as well as with the anomalies that took place in Arizona, ballots found/returned/counted long after the election ended have only benefited Democrats—a statistical impossibility in a fair system.

The Epoch Times reported[3] that "40 percent of the state's 12.5 million votes were counted after Nov. 6—a striking development, considering mail in ballots were once intended to assist those who couldn't physically vote in a polling booth due to disability, infirmity, or residing out of state, such as overseas military personnel." It appears, however, that that system is now being abused for political gain.

Rep. Mimi Walters, a Republican, carried a more than 6,000-vote lead[4] on election day, yet somehow lost by more than 12,500 votes[5] weeks after the election. In Orange County, Young Kim was actually elected the first Korean-American Congresswoman. That victory was short lived. "Her 14-point lead was the lone bright spot on an otherwise dismal night for Orange County Republicans. But, over the past week, Republicans have watched the first-generation immigrant's lead evaporate. With thousands of provisional ballots left to count, her commanding lead is now underwater. She lost one week after the election," wrote Shawn Steel[6], California committeeman for the Republican National Committee. "How does a 14-point Republican lead disappear? Merciless and unsparing, California Democrats have systematically undermined California's already-weak voter protection laws to guarantee permanent one-party rule." Steel continued in his op-ed and commented on two thorny issues pertaining to California's voting irregularities:

- **"Ballot Harvesting:** Is illegal in most states. But not California. As if it wasn't enough for every person to be automatically registered to vote and receive a ballot, Democrats have made it easier for their campaign operatives to collect those absentee ballots. Also in 2016, state lawmakers eliminated the ballot protection law that enabled only a trusted family member to return another voter's ballot. Assembly Bill 1921 now allows anyone to return an absentee ballot. The law has encouraged campaign operatives to engage in coercive tactics. One Democrat voter described coercive intimidation tactics employed by a Democrat campaign in a 2017 special election, leading even the liberal *Los Angeles Times* editorial board to criticize the law.
- **"Ballots Accepted Up to Week After Election Day:** In California, voting doesn't stop on Election Day. Absentee ballots need only be postmarked by Election Day, with ballots counted that arrive up to three days late. If ballots are sent to the wrong county, the ballot is valid for an additional four

days. As Mr. Mitchell points out, 'That means you literally have seven days after an election where a county could still be receiving legitimate ballots.'"

"In California, this will end up largely favoring candidates I would describe as 'establishment Democrats,' but I see no reason why Republicans will not take up this approach and use it to their advantage in certain districts as well. It is non-partisan in that this is basically about people in power making it easier for their favored candidates to win elections," he said.

When asked if there was any relationship to ballot harvesting and voter suppression, he said[7], "Voter suppression and ballot harvesting have a shared logic: they seek to manipulate election results on behalf of the powerful by manipulating vulnerable voters. Ultimately, we have a problem with low voter turnout, especially among the poor. There are many reasons for this, and not all the reasons are clear. But one potential reason is that too many people believe their vote doesn't matter in a rigged system."

He continued, "Ballot harvesting will contribute to that despair and cynicism. In that sense I believe it will ultimately directly suppress the vote. One of the darkest parts of living in this period of history is the feeling that democratic institutions are in decline. We have to stand by them. The legislature achieved the direct opposite with the bill on ballot harvesting."

The Wall Street Journal called[8] California's ballot harvesting initiative the "biggest score" for Democrats and a strategy that "is carefully designed to enhance Democratic turnout." The WSJ Editorial Board also said that ballot harvesting "creates opportunities for harvesters to "help" voters complete their ballots, or even pay to finish them, and it's easy for the unscrupulous to lose ballots they think may go for the wrong candidate. This is why ballot harvesting is illegal in many states…"

In response, a letter to the editor[9] from a former prosecutor named John E. Clark was written to the WSJ, explaining how California's lax laws create an environment that invites election fraud:

> *"As a former federal prosecutor who has investigated and prosecuted election fraud, I can vouch for the accuracy of your critique of California's voting model ("Harvesting Democratic Votes,[10]" Review & Outlook, Jan. 19). Most jurisdictions have long recognized that some absentee voting is necessary, but any ballot marked outside the supervised environment of an official polling place is potentially subject to undue influence or worse.*

> *"The first key to facilitating election fraud is getting names on the voter-registration list. The second key is controlling the votes cast in as many of those names as possible. Automatically registering persons regardless of any expression of interest is a significant step to empower fraud. Next, automatically mailing ballots to all who are registered substantially increases the opportunity. Finally,*

allowing any person to show up at homes and collect ballots essentially guarantees that fraud will occur.

"The basic technique of those who practice organized election fraud has been similar for ages, from notorious big-city political machines to equally notorious rural political bosses such as George Parr, who perpetrated the "Box 13" fraud in my state in 1948: Get as many names as possible on the registration list and then control the votes cast in as many of those names as possible. Under California's election laws, it won't require the iron-fisted control of a political boss or a powerful machine to improperly affect election outcomes. Registration is automatic, any ballot can be marked in unknown circumstances and any interested person can collect and deliver it (or not)."

While people across the country were apoplectic about the state's clear goal of unduly influencing the outcome of the 2016 midterm election, progressives in the state tried to simply shrug it off.

The *Los Angeles Times* Editorial Board penned its own piece[11] about ballot harvesting in the California midterms, calling the GOP response to harvesting "rubbish" and pleading with its readers, "To reiterate: There's absolute [sic] no reason to suspect fraud in last month's election." Yet, even after gaslighting their audience and labeling Republicans conspiracy theorists for suspecting fraud and saying there was no evidence that the law was misused, they conceded that the harvesting law "was written without sufficient safeguards and suspicions of abuse were inevitable."

They also acknowledged that ballot harvesting could be abused by people who are extremely aggressive, people who may just so happen to "lose" certain ballots and pay (or coerce) voters to hand over their unfilled mail ballots. They too concede that this is why states ban ballot harvesting or limit the number of ballots a third party can turn in.

But, because of the decentralized nature of our elections, with each state responsible for its own election laws and enforcement, there are glaring inconsistencies throughout the country on this issue. Ballot harvesting is completely legal in one jurisdiction, but against the law in others.

Take for instance the state of Arizona, which passed a law that banned ballot harvesting back in 2016. For context, there is clear animus against Republicans by Democrats in Arizona, with one left-leaning organization, The Arizona Advocacy Network, saying—without evidence—in 2015[12] that "when it comes to disenfranchising eligible voters, Arizona is, unfortunately, a national leader." This is the same group that recommended weakening state election laws by pushing for same-day registration, eliminating a requirement to show identification, counting votes that are cast/received after polling closes and allowing votes from precincts that people don't even live in, among other things. So, it should come as no surprise that any measure aimed at limiting ballot harvesting would face opposition.

After the Arizona ballot harvesting ban passed, Democrats issued immediate challenges to the law citing (drum-roll please) racism, arguing that it[13] "placed an unlawful burden on the right to vote and disproportionately affected minority voters, notably Native Americans." A district judge upheld the law, and the case was appealed to the Ninth Circuit Court of Appeals and ultimately ended up at the United States Supreme Court. But, in late October 2016, the Supreme Court sided with Arizona and issued an order allowing the state to enforce its ballot harvesting ban.

While this was seen as a win for conservatives out West, Republicans back East didn't fare so well.

In North Carolina, an operative for Republican Mark Harris's campaign conducted their own ballot harvesting operation in the 2018 midterms. The only problem was that in North Carolina, ballot harvesting is illegal. And there is a cruel irony in the fact that it was actually Republicans who banned it[14] in North Carolina.

Kim Strach, state elections director, held a hearing and said, "The evidence that we will provide today will show that a coordinated, unlawful and substantially resourced absentee ballot scheme operated in the 2018 general election.[15]"

On the first day of the hearing, a woman named Lisa Britt said that she was tasked with collecting ballots and was paid $125 per each 50 absentee ballots she collected. She said that she was paid by her former stepfather, Leslie McCrae Dowless, to collect the ballots. According to a CNN wire report[16], she also admitted "that she signed absentee ballots as a witness when she did not witness the voter filling it out. She also said she forged her mother's signature on between seven and nine ballots to 'not raise red flags' that the same people were signed as witnesses on too many absentee ballots."

It was also said[17] that Dowless approached voters who were high on drugs and accepted signed but blank ballots, for which those people were paid.

Dowless was arrested in February 2019 and indicted on charges related to the allegations of ballot harvesting. The Charlotte Observer reported[18] that "According to the indictment, Dowless 'unlawfully, willfully, and feloniously' submitted absentee ballots and concealed that they were not sent by voters. North Carolina law makes it a felony for anyone other than a voter's close relative to take possession of their absentee ballot."

Harris was never charged and had no knowledge of the scheme. *The Hill* quoted his testimony[19]: "Neither I nor any of the leadership in my campaign were aware of or condone the improper activities that have been testified to in this hearing," before reporting on witness statements that there was "lax oversight" by the Harris campaign over the ballot collecting initiative.

Despite holding a lead in votes cast, Harris was never certified as the winner because of the fraud allegations. He also called for a new election, to which the North Carolina Board of Elections agreed.

Shortly after the arrest was announced, Democrat Dan McCready (the candidate who was set to lose the election), wrote in a Tweet[20]: "From the moment the first vote was stolen in North Carolina, from the moment the first voice was silenced by election fraud, the people have deserved justice. Today was a great step forward for democracy in North Carolina."

His comments are rather fascinating, because he seems to be making an argument against the principle of ballot harvesting rather than the fact that it just so happens to be illegal in his state. Acknowledging that ballot harvesting produced "stolen" votes and freely admitting that this practice had "silenced" legitimate voices who were simply trying to exercise their civic duty clearly makes the case *against* ballot harvesting as an acceptable practice in general. And I basically agree with his final point: prosecuting anyone engaged in ballot harvesting *is* a great step forward (even though we are a constitutional republic, not a democracy).

North Carolina is a great case study on the inherent dangers of ballot harvesting and should prompt any jurisdiction currently allowing it or considering it to re-think this practice.

Steven F. Huefner, Professor in Law and Judicial Administration at The Ohio State University Moritz College of Law, wrote an article wherein he described at least three separate types of fraud that can occur when political operatives conduct ballot harvesting[21]:

1. "Those collecting ballots can intentionally discard (or conveniently lose or misplace) any ballots they suspect or know (perhaps even by opening the ballot envelopes) have been cast in favor of the 'wrong'

candidate(s).

2. "Those collecting the ballots can open the ballot envelopes and change or alter whatever votes the voter originally recorded.

3. "Those collecting the ballots can collect unvoted ballots (or partially voted ballots) and complete the ballots themselves."

He also notes that the "first two types of ballot harvesting fraud can occur without any wrongdoing on the part of the absentee voter." It's a system that relies on trust and the patently absurd notion that a political partisan actively working on a campaign will be acting in good faith when delivering ballots for their opponents, while they are largely unsupervised with no real accountability over the chain-of-custody of the ballots they're collecting. Would you really trust a hard-core Elizabeth Warren supporter who is picking up ballots in a red state, like Utah, or swing state, like Pennsylvania, to turn in Republican ballots if they could simply toss them into a dumpster and not get caught? Did people in North Carolina have their trust eviscerated by a GOP operative caught engaging in outright fraud after their ballots were collected? The casting of a ballot is not a civic duty that should be outsourced to others, except in the rarest of circumstances.

With the potential to simply discard undesirable ballots, ballot harvesting can effectively turn political operatives into the actual vote counters. One person, one vote? Good luck with that. Everything about this system flies in the face of a free society that trumpets fair elections.

Ballot harvesting fraud "can be especially difficult to detect and prevent," Huefner, who has worked in the U.S. Senate's Office of Legal Counsel advising on contested elections, said in his article. He also put a very fine point on this issue when he said, "No state should hesitate to make absentee ballot harvesting illegal, and to take steps to increase awareness and enforcement of this prohibition."

Real Clear Politics reported that ballot harvesting takes place in 19 states and that there is little to no information on its impact and abuses[22]. This means that nearly half of the country is potentially exposed to election fraud through this practice. Let's remember, many elections (including the 2016 presidential election) were decided by relatively small margins. It doesn't take a lot to swing a congressional seat or any other elected office with a type of fraud that is largely undetectable. This represents a clear threat to the sanctity of an individual's vote.

In November 2018, Montana became the latest state to pass an anti-ballot harvesting law. *The Associated Press* reported[23] that Republican Senator Al Olszewski "proposed the ban after two of his constituents in northwestern Montana complained of pushy ballot collectors coming to their homes."

"For a woman in her 70s that's maybe frail and lives alone and feels intimidated, at least now they can say 'please leave' and have confidence that the law is behind them," he told the AP.

The AP article also said that voting-rights advocates

were upset that anti-ballot harvesting laws were being passed without evidence of actual ballot fraud, but that was "before questions were raised about the activities in the North Carolina congressional race." They said that such measures punish voters without doing anything to "detect, deter or punish fraud."

This is the entirely wrong way to frame this issue, particularly in light of the irregularities that occurred during the 2018 midterms. Even in the absence of a preponderance of evidence of fraud, that large-scale fraud is possible and even likely though such a questionable practice is reason enough to ban it. No one is disenfranchised because a biased agent working for a political campaign can't come pick up their ballot. Every state provides myriad options for voting. And, as we will see with electronic voting, some election systems should be avoided entirely unless and until we are able to demonstrate an exceptionally high degree of confidence that such systems are secure and cannot be used fraudulently.

In March 2019, *Real Clear Politics* reported on a tweet[24] from Democratic National Committee Chairman Tom Perez that commented on the North Carolina ballot harvesting issue, which said, "Calling for a new election in #NC09 was the right decision. Americans shouldn't have to wonder if their votes will be counted. We need to fight like hell to make sure this doesn't happen again in #NC09 or anywhere else in our country." Perez had no such condemnation for the ballot harvesting that occurred in the progressive state of California.

The double standard actually couldn't be more clear: ballot harvesting is to be shunned when it helps Republicans, but completely acceptable when Democrats employ it. Good for me, but not for thee.

The Federalist reported on California's ballot harvesting, highlighting an encounter that was actually caught on video on a family's doorbell camera. "A harvester, identifying herself as Lulu, asks for Brandi, and says she is there to collect her ballot, explaining that there is 'this new service, but only to, like, people who are supporting the Democratic Party.'[25]"

But, although progressives in California took advantage of harvesting for their own gain, Republicans are beefing up their efforts to take advantage of the exact same system. And why shouldn't they?

The *Washington Post* reported[26] on statements made by Rep. Tom Emmer, chairman of the National Republican Congressional Committee, who commented on California's ballot harvesting efforts, saying, "While the Democrats had an operation on the ground that was actually doing the ballot harvesting, we did not have a corresponding organization that was doing that. That won't happen again."

The paper also mentioned a NRCC donor call, where political director Justin Richards vowed to fight fire with fire, saying that "being prepared for [ballot] harvesting" is a high priority for the GOP. "We're going to have the vote apparatus in place," he said.

From a political standpoint, it would behoove Republicans to step up efforts in this area wherever ballot harvesting is legal and employ the exact same strategies as Democrats, but with even more fervor and a larger political machine. If the rules of the game are allowed to be this loose, then both sides should have the ability to benefit accordingly.

In Florida, a 2016 investigation showed[27] that numerous "primary races uncovered significant evidence of voter fraud by Democratic candidates, who pushed back on any criticism by claiming racial discrimination." Three Democratic candidates, Mack Bernard, state Representative Al Jacquet and a candidate for state Senate, Bobby Powell, ordered mail ballots for constituents, in some cases without the constituents' knowledge or consent. They subsequently completed the ballots for their constituents, or the candidates stood in their constituents' homes with them while they completed the ballot. It just so happened that all of them won their elections because of the large number of absentee votes. The controversy resulted in a 10-month investigation by the Palm Beach County State Attorney's Office.

The *Palm Beach Post* reported[28] the county's Supervisor of Elections Susan Bucher stated that the investigation was concerning "a group of subjects that were working for certain political campaigns that were involved in voter fraud" via absentee and vote-by-mail ballots. It was reported that she suspected "that as many as 2,000 absentee ballots and ballot requests could be fraudulent." The investigation found several troubling things: a large number of voters received absentee ballots that were never requested, more than two dozen signatures on absentee ballot request forms appeared to be forged and an unnamed man was spotted on security camera footage dropping off large numbers of absentee ballot request forms to the Elections Supervisor's Office.

For some unknown reason, detectives didn't even bother to interview the three candidates and no formal charges were ever brought, leaving a cloud of suspicion over all three races.

In a separate case in Madison County, Florida dating back to 2011, eight people were charged with election fraud and the County Elections Supervisor Jada Woods Williams was charged with 17 counts of willful neglect of duty for allowing the distribution of those absentee ballots, contrary to Florida state statute. Woods and her husband were "accused of asking voters to get absentee ballot request forms and then writing in different mailing addresses where the ballots were to be mailed," reported[29] the *Tampa Bay Times*. Investigators found that people picked up more ballots than allowed by law and that 80 different ballots were sent to just nine addresses.

According to the State of Florida's website[30]:

> *Abra "Tina" Hill Johnson, 43, was charged with 10 counts of fraud in connection with casting a vote, and two counts of absentee ballots and voting violations. Her husband Ernest Sinclair Johnson, Jr., 45, was charged with 11 counts of fraud in connection with casting votes, one count of corruptly influencing voting, and one count of per-*

jury by false written declaration.

The following individuals, all residents of Madison, Fla., were arrested for their role in the fraud:

Judy Ann Crumitie, 51, charged with four counts of fraud in connection with casting a vote, and one count of providing a false report to law enforcement authorities

Laverne V. Haynes, 57, charged with two counts of fraud in connection with casting a vote, two counts of perjury by false written declaration, and one count of providing a false report to law enforcement authorities

Ora Bell Rivers, 41, charged with seven counts of fraud in connection with casting a vote, three counts of perjury by false written declaration, and one count of providing a false report to law enforcement authorities

Raven Simona Williams, 20, charged with two counts of fraud in connection with casting a vote, two counts of perjury by false written declaration, and one count of providing a false report to law enforcement authorities

Shalonda Michaelle Brinson, 36, charged with nine counts of fraud in connection with casting a vote, and one count of provided a false report to law enforcement authorities.

Also, in 2011, 12 Democrats were charged with voter fraud in Georgia for using absentee ballots to fraudulently vote in a bitter November 2010 school board election in Brooks County in which the final tally was changed by an unusually large wave of absentee ballots," reported[31] *The Daily Caller*. "What I have seen in my state, in my region, is the most aggressive practitioners of voter fraud are local machines who are tied lock, stock and barrel to the special interests in their communities—the landfills, the casino operators—and they're cooking the [ballot] boxes on election day, they're manufacturing absentee ballots, they're voting [in the names of] people named Donald Duck because they want to control politics and thwart progress," former Alabama Democratic Rep. Artur Davis told *Daily Caller*. He also said that voter ID laws are what's needed to counter fraud in elections.

In a separate incident the same year, a jury in Tunica County, Mississippi convicted an NAACP official on 10 separate counts of fraudulently casting absentee ballots. She voted in the names of six living people and four dead people. *The Daily Caller* reported[32] that Lessadolla Sowers "received a five-year prison term for each of the 10 counts, but Circuit Court Judge Charles Webster permitted Sowers to serve those terms concurrently, according to the Tunica Times, the only media outlet to cover the sentencing." Yet even despite all of this and a member of the NAACP being convicted of voter fraud, NAACP President Benjamin Jealous still managed to attack a Mississippi law that required voters to show ID, calling it an attempt to[33] disenfranchise minorities through some "of the last existing legal pillars of Jim Crow."

In a 2016 Democratic primary for the Missouri House of Representatives, Bruce Franks was leading and on election day managed to win the primary by a margin of just 90 votes. However, his challenger, Rep. Penny Hubbard (once called[34] "a member of a St. Louis political dynasty known for ballot harvesting") managed to produce 142 absentee ballots that upended that election and handed it to her instead. But, the results got tossed out and a new election was ordered, as the 142 absentee ballots were not delivered in sealed envelopes.

Dave Roland, attorney for Franks, also cited numerous other irregularities and said that at least 238 other votes should have been rejected. The St. Louis Post-Dispatch said that[35] "Franks received nearly 53 percent of votes cast at the polls on the day of the election, but Hubbard won 78.5 percent of the absentee ballots, giving her a 90-vote advantage in the final tabulation."

The biggest problem with ballot harvesting is that there is no chain of custody. It is often impossible to certify the authenticity of the ballot, the signature or to know where the ballots even came from that are being dropped off. As trial lawyer Robert Barnes wrote on Twitter[36], ballot harvesting will "allow anybody to walk into an elections office and hand over truckloads of vote by mail envelopes with ballots inside, no questions asked, no verified records kept. It amounts to an open invitation to large-scale vote buying, voter coercion." In 2014, *The Gateway Pundit* reported on a case that appears to be exactly that, when an official in Arizona caught a man stuffing hundreds[37] of early ballots into a ballot box. A 2012 Caltech/MIT Voting Technology Project report[38] highlighted the obvious risk associated with this process: "Having tens of millions of ballots being transmitted and marked without strict chain-of-custody procedures creates risks that simply do not exist with any form of in-person voting, whether on Election Day or in early-voting settings."

Many suspect that the large numbers of ballots that magically turn up after elections are filled out by political operatives rather than actual voters. Political consultant Aaron Harris confirmed that theory, telling *CBS News*[39] that "harvesters sit around and fill these out by the hundreds, often by the thousands." This is likely how states like Florida and California magically produce 250,000 ballots[40], deliver them at the last minute and overturn legitimate elections. Harris also showed multiple documents of signatures that didn't match on applications and envelopes. He was interviewed for a story about four women who were indicted in Tarrant County Texas, for obtaining mail-in ballots and filling them out for Democratic Party candidates in 2016. All four women were charged[41] with felonies.

Though ballot harvesting exacerbates the potential for fraud, even without it, both absentee and mail-in ballots present challenges.

For instance, in 2017 elderly voters in West Dallas said that someone was forging their signatures on mail-in ballots. This prompted officials in Texas to take action, including drafting legislation to prevent mail-in ballot fraud that was taking place at nursing homes throughout the state. Rather than have private individuals or political operatives picking up ballots, the law would task election judges with delivering and collecting mail-in ballots at nursing homes and similar facilities, when five or more absentee ballots are requested. *The Dallas News* reported that the new process would protect seniors—some of America's most vulnerable people—by preventing[42] "political operatives from requesting mail-in ballots for unsuspecting seniors or the infirm and then returning to the facility to pick up the ballots before they reach the voter. It would also make it unnecessary for a person other than an election judge to help a nursing home resident vote." Also, in San Antonio, TX, a criminal investigation was launched[43] after the 2018 primary election had several people report that mail-in ballots had been filled out in their names.

According to the Texas Secretary of State[44], a voter in Texas is only eligible to vote by mail by meeting four specific criteria:

- Be 65 years or older
- Be disabled
- Be out of the county on election day and during the period for early voting by personal appearance
- Be confined in jail, but otherwise eligible

If more states adopted similar measures, it would be a significant step to helping to reduce the potential for voter fraud. However, for various reasons, some states are pursuing the opposite.

Multiple counties in Nebraska are switching[45] to all-mail elections after encountering staffing shortages at polling places. They're not alone. Nebraska counties are joining 22 other states that allow some elections to be conducted entirely via mail. The National Conference of State Legislatures (NCSL) said[46], "This does not preclude in-person voting opportunities on and/or before Election Day." Other states that allow all-mail voting include Alaska, Arkansas, California, Colorado, Florida, Hawaii, Idaho, Kansas, Maryland, Minnesota, Missouri, Montana, Nebraska, Nevada, New Jersey, New Mexico, North Dakota, Oregon, Utah, Washington and Wyoming.

But, as we've seen throughout this chapter, making voting more convenient doesn't necessarily translate into higher participation, considering that oftentimes millions of people don't even have their vote counted as a result. The National Election Defense Coalition[47] cited a study by a political scientist named Charles Stewart III, who determined that voting-by-mail had a failure rate of roughly 21% in the 2008 election, stating:

- Of 35.5 million voters who requested absentee ballots, only 27.9 million were actually counted
- Nearly 4 million ballots requested by voters never even reached them
- Nearly 3 million ballots received by voters never made it back to election officials

- Election officials rejected 800,000 ballots

In 2016, California launched a new system that allowed counties to switch to all mail-in ballot elections, even providing prepaid postage. The *Sacramento Bee* reported[48] the state also "added pre-registration for 16- and 17-year-olds, created conditional registration up until Election Day, expanded the languages in which voting material is available, tightened the restrictions for removing somebody from the voter rolls, and allowed anybody to turn in a mail ballot if it is signed by the voter." Under the guise of expanding access to the polls to supposedly counteract past suppression, the state is leading the way in creating a system catastrophically ripe for fraud.

Also in 2016, in Fort Worth, Texas, the State Attorney General launched an investigation into ballot harvesting thought to be[49] the "largest case of voter fraud the AG's office has ever investigated." Townhall reported:

> *"The perpetrators order mail-in ballots by forging the names of citizens in target districts. They then hire kindly middle-aged and older women to go door-to-door with those ballots in hand. They knock on the door of the citizen whose ballot they have, and make fraudulent claims as to why they are visiting. They may claim they are gathering signatures for a petition, or beg for a signature so they might 'meet their quota' for whatever alleged cause they are soliciting on behalf of. Frequently, it is something like 'Republicans are trying to take away the rights of*

black voters.'

"The citizen then unknowingly signs the yellow ballot carrier envelope that contains their ballot—a ballot the perpetrators have already filled out that supports their candidate.

"In other cases, the harvesters will appear with the citizen's ballot and ask if they need any help filling it out. As they already have the voter's historical voting record, they will say something like, 'You normally vote all Democrat, right?'—even though it is usually a democrat primary or non partisan municipal elections which they are 'helping' them with—and proceed to fill out the ballot as desired by the perpetrators.

"The harvesting scheme takes advantage of the most vulnerable citizens: the elderly, the uneducated, those who don't speak English as a first language, those in lower income brackets. In cases where the voter resides in a minority neighborhood, a minority harvester is hired to do the dirty work."

Woody Hayes, legendary football coach at The Ohio State University, used to say that when you pass the ball, three things can happen and two of them are bad. The same applies to ballot harvesting. If our country is to be serious about ensuring safe and secure elections, a great step forward is to stop caving to pressure from political reprobates and relegate ballot harvesting to the ash heap of history.

CHAPTER 6

Voter I.D. & Voter Suppression

"The data do not support the notion that the 'brown-brown' are too dumb, too lazy or otherwise incapable of obtaining the necessary identification to vote."

— *Larry Elder*

Noam Chomsky is referenced[1] as stating, "The smart way to keep people passive and obedient is to strictly limit the spectrum of acceptable opinion, but allow very lively debate within that spectrum—even encourage the more critical and dissident views. That gives people the sense that there's free thinking going on, while all the time the presuppositions of the system are being reinforced by the limits put on the range of the debate." This idea is similar to a phenomenon referred to as the Overton Window. This phenomenon, named after Joseph P. Overton, refers to the limited range of ideas politicians can pursue without seeming too extreme for the general public. The Mackinac Center for Public Policy says[2], "The core concept is that politicians are limited in what policy ideas they can support—they generally only pursue policies that are widely accepted throughout society as legitimate policy options. These policies lie inside the Overton Window. Other policy ideas exist, but politicians risk losing popular support if they champion these ideas." While Overton acknowledges the existence of this spectrum, Chomsky suggests that this spectrum can be artificially manipulated and controlled in order to produce or prevent specific policy outcomes. We see this in action in discussion and debate around election fraud, specifically with regard to how the two major political parties approach this topic. Language is always used that frames the conversation around two assumptions: Republicans are trying to make voting more difficult and Democrats are trying to make voting easier. These are false and arbitrary limits.

The real discussion is not about who is trying to make voting more or less easy but who is trying to make elections more secure and who is introducing increased opportunities for fraud. But, by intentionally limiting discussion to "easy" versus "harder," the spectrum of acceptable thought is greatly limited. Reasonable policies can be summarily dismissed if those recommending them can be falsely maligned as being motivated by disenfranchising sects of voters.

The demagoguery of Republicans over voter and election integrity—through the misplaced and overuse of now-banal terms like "voter suppression"—is simply a public relations tool.

It's becoming increasingly difficult to have a rational conversation about election fraud without some political partisan throwing rhetorical Molotov cocktails into the conversation. That's exactly what happens when the phrase "voter suppression" is violently tossed around. In America, it's now vogue to paint with broad strokes and have such an aversion to facts and logic that we can literally make anything we want equate to voter suppression. Didn't bother to register on time? Voter suppression. Ineligible to vote? Voter suppression. Server forgot to order your hamburger without cheese? Voter suppression. For the low, low price of $5.99, *anything* and *everything* can be deemed voter suppression.

Actual voter suppression has been defined as any action or policy that has the effect of discouraging or preventing individuals or groups of people from voting. The underlying assumption is that those people are *legal* voters. But, in today's politically charged climate, when someone claims "voter suppression" is taking place, what they are actually doing in many cases is labeling their opponents as racist. In political conversations, calling someone racist is now an effective means to shut down dialogue and debate. Part of the reason that America is unable to fully account for all of the election fraud that is clearly taking place is because efforts to stymie fraud are opposed under the guise of racism, using the term "voter suppression" as a proxy.

One of the easiest ways to prevent illegal voting is to require government-issued identification to cast a ballot. Yet, for the Left, the mere prospect of requiring photo identification to vote elicits explosive reactions and accusations that doing so would disenfranchise black and brown voters, a theme you have already seen throughout this book. Some even go so far as to liken showing ID to poll taxes, comparing a responsible policy to one of the darkest eras in America's past.

The Brookings Institute has argued[3] that "more stringent photo identification requirements have become the new 'poll tax' for more than 21 million Americans, or 11 percent of the entire voting-eligible population without government-issued photo IDs."

"Poll taxes belong to an ugly chapter in U.S. race relations," wrote Charles Postel[4] of *Politico*. "They were part of the Southern states' Jim Crow system, which prevailed from the late 19th century into the 1960s, and robbed blacks and other minorities of their political and civil rights."

The 15th amendment to the Constitution says[5]: "The right of citizens of the United States to vote shall not be denied or abridged by the United States or by any State on account of race, color, or previous condition of servitude." Unhappy with black men having the right to vote, several states instituted poll taxes in the south as a barrier to the polls. It was done specifically to keep certain people from being able to exercise their legal right to vote. It is not a fair comparison to equate poll taxes with requiring photo ID, which aims to ensure that only legal citizens are casting ballots.

It can be reasonably inferred that Former Attorney General Eric Holder would understand this. So, for an esteemed member of the U.S. government to tap into such a dark, painful, emotional place and use such incendiary language to falsely draw parallels to this policy is disturbing. In 2017, Holder spoke at a luncheon for the NAACP and said[6] that the "right to vote is under siege" and that the Republican Party was on the wrong side of history. Holder's comments illuminate the language used against people who simply want to secure our elections.

Just a few months earlier, Holder spoke[7] at Al Sharpton's National Action Network convention and said that minorities were "under siege" by renewed calls for voter identification laws.

In 2019, Holder's race baiting continued on Dean Obeidallah's SiriusXM radio show. He stated[8]—without evidence—that "voter suppression is worse than it has been" and "people are trying to take our vote away." He went on to say, "If we have a fair system, progressives and Democrats will beat the hell out of Republicans and conservatives, in a fair system." Then, Holder engaged in projection by stating, "They only win by cheating. And so we have to be prepared to fight." One thing that should be obvious to most by now is that Democrats have a bad habit of accusing Republicans of doing what Democrats are actually doing. Holder's gaslighting of his audience is a perfect example. As you've already read, there are many examples of cheating and election fraud, and with the vast majority of the offenses, the beneficiaries just happen to be Democrats. The idea that the fight against Republicans is anything other than a contrived attempt to prevent transparency to keep the con going is laughable.

The Left in America has long insinuated that black people are so incredibly helpless, broke and stupid that we couldn't possibly figure out how to get identification. They are so committed to this patronizing attitude that in 2016, *The Washington Post* actually ran a story[9] with the headline "Getting a photo ID so you can vote is easy. Unless you're poor, black, Latino or elderly." The piece attempts to grab you emotionally right from the beginning, opening with a story of Anthony Settles, an older man who has an expired Texas identification card, a social security card and an old student ID—none of which qualified him to vote in Texas in 2016. He needed a current identification card. Also, he changed his name back in 1964 and needed to show his name change certificate from 1964 in order to get a new ID card. Because it was so long ago, neither he nor his attorneys were able to produce the required documentation. Settles was able to get a new document with his updated name, but the cost of going to court and going through this process was more than $250—a cost he wouldn't pay in order to vote. All this being said, this case is clearly an exception not the rule.

"It has been a bureaucratic nightmare," Settles told the *Washington Post*. He got over his skis when he said, "The intent of this law is to suppress the vote. I feel like I am not wanted in this state." Most people don't have such hurdles when it comes to verifying who they are. In Settles' case specifically, those hurdles were created by the man himself, not some repressive system of tyranny, hell-bent on depriving him of his right to vote. Playing the victim might get you a feature in a left-leaning newspaper, but it lends zero credibility to the narrative that you're being systematically disenfranchised, simply because you didn't have the interest in obtaining or maintaining proper identification. As you've already seen through this book, Texas has had ongoing issues with voter fraud and illegal names on its voter rolls. It therefore has a vested interest in making sure that those who vote are who they say they are.

The *Post* reported that roughly "11 percent of Americans do not have government-issued photo identification cards, such as a driver's license or a passport" and the contention is that those who don't tend to be racial minorities or elderly. In 2012, *Slate* tackled this issue, saying[10], "Minorities are less likely to have driver's licenses because they are more likely to be poor and to live in urban areas. If you can't afford a car, or if you don't need one because you take the bus or subway, you are less likely to have a driver's license." What they leave out is the fact that other IDs (like a state identification card) are easy to obtain and are also inexpensive. Even if you don't drive, you can find a way to the local DMV and get a state ID. I spoke with an election worker in North Carolina who told me that prior to the 2016 election, the North Carolina GOP actually offered to drive anyone who needed ID to vote to the DMV. Only two people accepted the rather generous offer. Why? Because (as they emphatically told me) most people (yes, even black people) do have ID. And, if voting is critically important to an individual, they will have no trouble obtaining one of the various forms of acceptable ID required by their state. (*Note: Texas offered seven different types of acceptable forms of identification.*) Elections don't take place on a weekly basis. A considerable amount of time is given between elections and, if they really want to vote, any reasonable person is capable of getting what's needed in order to verify who they are and cast a ballot.

The persistent assertion by Democrats/progressives that blacks are, by and large, unable to figure out how to get an ID is incredibly patronizing. But hey, don't take my word for it; take the word of a random sample of black people who were surveyed in Harlem when asked about ID policies for voting.

In a video entitled[11] "How white liberals really view black voters", Ami Horowitz, writer, filmmaker and producer, interviewed white liberals in Berkeley, California and blacks in Harlem to better understand their thoughts on the issue of voter ID. The video is shocking.

"Do you have an opinion on voter ID laws?" he asks a random young Berkeley woman at the beginning of the video. She responds, "Uh, yeah, they're usually pretty racist." Another young lady answered, saying, "I think voter ID laws are a way to perpetuate racism." He found a young man in sunglasses and asked him if voter ID laws suppressed the African American vote. The young man said, "Definitely. Because, they're less likely to have state IDs." Another young man, wearing a University of California Berkeley t-shirt said, "These type of people don't live in areas with easy access to DMVs or other places where they can get identification."

Arguably the most revealing statements about why obtaining ID is so overwhelming came from a man in a red sweater and the woman featured after him. Horowitz asked, "You can always get IDs, you can do [that] over the internet. Does that also make it difficult for black people in particular?" The man responded, "Yeah you have to have access to the internet. You have to be able to pay an internet service provider for certain fees," suggesting that blacks were too poor to be able to afford internet service. He then asked a young lady if she too felt like it was hard for black people to go online to figure out how to obtain an ID. She said, "Well I feel like they don't have the knowledge of how it works," suggesting we're just too stupid.

Horowitz's video then cut to him asking questions to blacks in Harlem about the difficulty of obtaining proper identification to vote, saying, "Now I'm here in East Harlem to ask black people their thoughts on what you just heard." The black men and women in Harlem were shocked at how progressives viewed them. "Do you carry ID?" he asked a black woman. "Yes I do," she responded. He asked, "Do you know any black person who doesn't carry ID?" She replied, "No. Why would they think we don't have ID?"

Another young man said, "I have my ID and my friends have their IDs, so we know what we need to carry around."

A separate black man in a bandana responded to Horowitz, saying, "Yeah, everybody I know has ID. That's one of the things you need to walk around New York with, an ID." Horowitz followed up with, "I heard a lot also that black people can't figure out how to get to the DMV. What's that say to you?" The man replied, "I know where it's at, it's on 125th street."

Horowitz asked a young black woman in sunglasses, "Do you know any black adult who does not have ID?" She replied, "No I don't." Horowitz replied, "Is it a weird thing to even say that?" She answered, "Yes it is."

Highlighting the complete lunacy of this issue, when Horowitz began speaking with a couple on this issue, a man sporting a goatee replied, "What is this, some type of trick candid camera or something like that?" right before he and the lady pulled out their IDs to show Horowitz. When he asked them, "Do you know where the DMV is around here?" the man said, "It's on 125th street and third avenue, I believe." Horowitz asked, "You know how to get there?" The man said, "Yeah." Horowitz asked, "You have a problem getting there if you need to get there?" The man said, "No."

When Horowitz asked three people what their perception was of people who felt this way about blacks, all answered by saying it is "ignorant" of them. One lady took it a step further, saying, "I think it is a little racist, because you're putting people in a category and you have no idea what you're talking about."

When told what "liberals" think of blacks' inability to obtain ID, another black woman said, "What people are they talking to? Who are these people talking to?"

Finally, Horowitz asked all of the black respondents in Harlem if they would have a problem with a rule saying you must show your ID before you vote and, lo and behold, not a single person took issue with it. Not one.

We have two worlds that exist on this topic: one that progressive politicians and activists say exists and the real world. If you listen to propaganda from the Left, the task of showing proper ID to cast a ballot is a racist, debilitating request, which disenfranchises the black segment of the population; if you ask black people themselves about showing ID, most of us don't seem to care.

For decades, we have been forced to watch political opportunists constantly pull these boogeymen out of the closet and pretend that black people have to be afraid of something that isn't even real. Anyone who dares to take an active role in shining a light on these issues and showing the community *en masse* that these ghosts don't really exist is immediately and mercilessly slandered. Blacks are largely viewed as property of the Left; just cogs in a political machine. In many ways, we are loved by progressives only to the extent that we can solidify their long-term grasp on power, which is why—even with decades of new black progressive leaders popping up—the outcomes in black neighborhoods in progressive districts rarely see the change they need. They use fear to manipulate blacks into supporting their policies and backing them in elections, guaranteeing themselves a permanent voting bloc. Claims that blacks are unable to obtain proper identification is simply an extension of this incredibly disparaging and paternalistic pathology.

Voter ID should be mandatory in all states for any citizen who wants to vote in U.S. elections. We have to show ID to buy alcohol, cigarettes, apply for welfare and food stamps, check into a hotel, drive a car, get married, adopt a pet, get on an airplane, open a bank account, donate blood, hold a rally protesting the orange man in the White House, purchase nail polish at CVS and to rent or buy a home[12]. It is almost impossible to participate in modern society without having identification. The only people who would be disenfranchised by Voter ID laws are illegal and ineligible voters.

Watchdog group Project Veritas (PV) attended a Christmas Party for the United Federation of Teachers back in 2015. Alan Schulkin, New York City Commissioner of Board of Elections, was in attendance. PV had a hidden camera and recorded him openly discussing the rampant voter fraud taking place in his state. Here's a partial transcript of that conversation[13]:

Schulkin: I think there is a lot of voter fraud. Right. Like I say, people don't realize certain neighborhoods in particular, they bus people around to vote.

PV: They do what?

Schulkin: *They bus them around. They put them in a bus and go poll site to poll site.*

PV: *Like, what kind of neighborhoods?*

Schulkin: *Well, I don't wanna say.*

PV: *Oh, like minority neighborhoods, like black neighborhoods and Hispanic neighborhoods?*

Schulkin: *And Chinese too.*

PV: *Oh, why do they do that, just to get more votes for Democrats?*

Schulkin: *For votes. More votes for themselves. They're all running for office.*

PV: *New York doesn't have voter ID laws, right? New York?*

Schulkin: *No, you can't, you cannot ask...they can't ask for voter ID.*

PV: *Why's that? They can't...*

Schulkin: *It's the law. The law says you can't ask for anything, which they really should be able to do. You know, I don't think it's too much to ask somebody to show some kind of an ID.*

PV: *Yeah, I mean why not? I mean you have to show an ID for everything else.*

Schulkin: Right. You go into a building you have to show them your ID.

PV: And you're saying there's a lot of absentee ballot fraud too.

Schulkin: Oh, there's thousands of absentee ballots. I don't know where they came from.

PV: Yeah but, that's the thing though, Hillary Clinton doesn't support voter ID laws.

Schulkin: I know, that's why I'm not always crazy about everything the Democrats do either. [New York City Mayor] de Blasio just gave out ID cards.

PV: He what?

Schulkin: He gave out ID cards, de Blasio. They don't...that's in lieu of a driver's license, but you can use it for anything. But they didn't vet the people to see who they really are. Anybody can go in there and say, I am Joe Smith, I want an ID card. It's absurd. There is a lot of fraud, not just voter fraud, all kinds of fraud.

In his local area alone, Schulkin saw immense fraud—groups of people being bussed around to polling locations, gross abuse of the absentee voting system and credentials that can be used for voting handed out indiscriminately like

Halloween candy. Lax voter ID laws are what make it all possible.

The following year, in 2016, PV recorded on hidden camera another political operative, Scott Foval, who was openly discussing illegal strategies that would be used to rig the election in favor of Hillary Clinton. (It's worth nothing that major news organizations declined to run the story, telling PV they were afraid of retaliation from a newly elected Clinton administration, given that she was widely expected to win.)

"We did it to them when we were in charge too. We did the exact same thing. Only, we manipulated the vote with money and action, not with laws," Foval said[14]. "It's a very easy thing for Republicans to say, 'Well they're bussing people in.' Well you know what? We've been bussing people in to deal with you fucking assholes for fifty years and we're not going to stop now, we're just going to find a different way to do it."

Foval then explains that he grew up with this idea, as he told the PV journalist that if they needed to, the Democratic party would bus people out to Iowa to vote. If there's any question as to his awareness of the illegality of these types of actions, he provides a straight answer.

"When I do this I think as an investigator first," he said. "I used to do the investigations, a different...method. I think backwards from how they would prosecute if they could, and then try to build out the method to avoid that." These statements were made just prior to discussing a plan on how to bring in voters from a different state to vote in the election, a rather diabolical way to increase turnout. Voter ID laws could certainly reduce this type of illegal turnout. But, do they have a similar effect on the overall turnout for legal voters?

Contrary to scare mongers on the Left, the data show that voter ID laws don't suppress voter turnout. In fact, the opposite is true. Voter ID laws preceded Barack Obama's 2008 election, and in places like Georgia and Indiana, minority turnout increased after the laws were passed. "It so happens that black voter turnout surpassed white turnout for the first time on record in 2012, even while more and more states were implementing these supposedly racist voter ID laws," said Jason Riley in his book[15], *Please Stop Helping Us: How Liberals Make It Harder for Blacks to Succeed*. Riley cited the U.S. Census Bureau, stating that blacks were the only race or ethnic group to show a significant increase in voting between 2008 and 2012. "Black voter turnout in 2012 surpassed white turnout by statistically significant margins in Florida, Virginia and the Carolinas, as well as in states with the strictest voter ID laws, such as Tennessee, Georgia, and Indiana," Riley wrote. "Democrats claim [voter ID] laws deny blacks the franchise" but the evidence does not support it.

In 2012, Edward Foley, executive director of an election law center at The Ohio State University Moritz College of Law, spoke about the implementation of voter ID laws and told the Atlanta Journal-Constitution[16], "It hasn't had the voter-suppressing effect that some people feared."

Also in 2012, researchers found[17] that in Tennessee and Virginia, "voter ID requirements did not negatively impact voter turnout, and may have actually increased turnout."

Time after time, all across the country, we find that even with strict voter ID requirements, there is no suppressive effect to the black vote.

In 2019, *The Daily Signal* reported[18] that the "National Bureau of Economic Research found that between 2008 and 2016, voter ID laws had 'no negative effect on registration or turnout, overall or for any specific group defined by race, gender, age or party affiliation.'"

In a 2005 report, former U.S. Secretary of State James Baker perfectly summed up this issue when he said[19], "The electoral system cannot inspire public confidence if no safeguards exist to deter or detect fraud or to confirm the identity of voters. Photo IDs currently are needed to board a plane, enter federal buildings, and cash a check. Voting is equally important."

There are some studies that purport to show that identification requirements do result in lower turnout for minorities. But, as the Heritage Foundation shows[20], they are flawed:

> *"The debunked Wisconsin study is, unfortunately, not alone in misusing the data for political gain. A January 2017 study by three professors from the University of California San Diego and Bucknell University—frequently referenced in liberal media outlets—is another unfortunate example. The study erroneously claims that*

voter-ID laws have a disparate impact on minorities and "diminish the participation of Democrats and those on the left, while doing little to deter the vote of Republicans and those on the right." This sensational finding generated a media storm, with the help of several opinion pieces from the authors making the politically charged (and false) claim that voter-ID laws "lower minority turnout and benefit the Republican Party."

"But these claims, too, were recently debunked by a group of professors from Yale, Stanford, and the University of Pennsylvania. Upon examining the data in the original study, the group found "no definitive relationship between strict voter ID laws and turnout." It also found that the original study contained measurement errors, omitted-variable bias, and misinterpreted data.

"In reality, then, such studies are designed to obscure the truth. The Heritage Foundation has published numerous papers looking at turnout data in states that implemented voter-ID laws. All of those studies show that ID require-ments do not keep voters from the polls, and that some states have even seen increases in turnout after their ID laws went into effect."

The Heritage Foundation highlighted the need for a better verification system, saying: "Voter-fraud convictions in-clude everything from impersonation fraud and false regis-trations to ineligible voting by felons and non-citizens.

American voter fraud continues apace, and the United States remains one of the only democracies in the world without a uniform requirement for voter identification." These facts stand in sharp contrast to the lie that President Obama told in 2017 when he said, right before leaving office, that the U.S. is "the only country among advanced democracies that makes it harder to vote." Any thoughts on what came next? (One more time for the people in the back: RACISM!) "It traces directly back to Jim Crow and the legacy of slavery," he said.

Despite Obama's lies about other nations not requiring ID to vote, The *National Review* reported[21] that most democracies worldwide require photo identification in order to vote "to prevent fraud and duplicate votes at the polls." When foreign leaders study the U.S. system of voting, they're perplexed. As part of a program by the International Foundation for Electoral Systems (IFES), election officials from more than 60 different countries came to the U.S. to observe how we conduct our presidential elections. The IFES website says[22] that it is a global organization that "engages with critical issues in democracy, governance and elections around the world." They pride themselves on "innovative work to provide citizens around the world with the fundamental human right to have a say in how they are governed." When they brought world leaders to view the U.S. election process, they were stunned by how lax our election security is.

"What's very unique about the way the Americans do it, it's not the process, it's the confidence that's placed in the process," said Sara Al-Utaibi[23], IFES deputy country director in Jordan. A Libyan official told[24] *Foreign Policy* that our system was shocking, because it relies on "trust and the good faith of election officials and voters." *Foreign Policy* noted several key areas of concern to international observers:

- No identification is required in much of the U.S.
- There are no police present at polling locations
- We have no uniform voting procedure (i.e., each state may have completely different rules and procedures)
- We don't have observers to ensure the rules and laws are being followed
- The provisional ballot system, where unregistered voters can vote anyway and verify their eligibility later
- Chain of custody issues: ballots are sent directly to poll workers and the handling of ballots, after voting, is entrusted to poll workers

Even some of the most repressive places around the world secure their elections better than does the U.S. And the concerns listed above are shared by the people within the U.S. fighting to close loopholes that can allow our elections to be compromised.

Even America's neighbor to the south, Mexico, has a national voter ID card, along with requirements and restrictions that are far more conservative that those that have been proposed in the U.S. The Brennan Center said[25] that "from November 1990 to July 1991" Mexico compiled its voter list from scratch by going door to door, visiting "16.5 million homes multiple times to register eligible citizens." Ultimately, their voter roll contained nearly 40 million voters. Unlike the U.S. system, in Mexico new voters have to show up to an election office in person, fill out a registration form, provide their fingerprint, provide a signature and have a photo taken for their voter ID card. The processing time for the card takes roughly 20 days, and voters must show valid identification to even pick up their voter ID card.

Can you imagine the outcry, allegations of civil rights violations and never-ending barrage of lawsuits if President Trump or anyone in the GOP recommended such solutions for the U.S.? But, lawsuits and court battles are now used as political weapons and are oftentimes overseen by activist judges with political aims of their own. Some of those cases make it all the way to the highest court in the land.

In 2008, the U.S. Supreme Court heard a case on voter ID. Indiana had recently passed a law requiring voter ID in order to cast a ballot. Prior to that[26], "Indiana identified voters by comparing signatures collected at the polling places with photocopied signatures on file." The photo ID had to meet four criteria[27] to be considered acceptable:

1) Display your photo, 2) Display your name, which must conform to your voter registration record, 3) Display an expiration date and either be current or have expired sometime after the date of the last General Election and 4) Be

issued by the State of Indiana of the U.S. government. Student IDs from private schools are not considered acceptable, but student IDs from Indiana State schools could be used as long as they meet the four criteria above. Anyone who was not able to show ID would have to cast a provisional ballot. They would then have until noon[28] 10 days after the election to follow up with the County Election Board and either provide photo ID or affirm one of the law's exemptions applies to them.

The Electronic Privacy Information Center (EPIC) said[29], "Two cases were filed in the U.S. District Court for the Southern District of Indiana challenging the new voter photo ID requirements." One of them was *Crawford v. Marion County Election Board*, which was filed by the ACLU and NAACP. Indiana's position was that verifying a voter's identity before allowing them to cast a ballot was a reasonable step in combating voter fraud. Crawford and the Indiana Democratic Party stated an oft used line[30] that "a voter photo ID requirement would disenfranchise the poor and the elderly, because they are the most likely to be without the means to pay for or the papers required to buy a government-issued photo ID document." They also said[31] that "the law substantially burdens the 'fundamental' right to vote, discriminates between and among different classes of voters, and disproportionately affects disadvantaged and minority voters." These are literally the same arguments we hear today.

The case was argued all the way up to the U.S. Supreme Court. The *Washington Post* quoted Justice Samuel A.

Alito Jr. as saying[32] during argument, "If [voter fraud] is not a problem at all, how do you account for the fact that the Commission on Federal Election Reform ... recommended a voter ID requirement, and many other countries around the world have voter ID requirements?" The Court ruled in a 6 - 3 vote in favor of the State of Indiana and upheld the voter ID law. *The New York Times* reported, "[The Supreme Court declared] that a requirement to produce photo identification is not unconstitutional and that the state has a 'valid interest' in improving election procedures as well as deterring fraud." And again, none of the claims that voter ID discriminated against or created an undue burden on voters proved true. But, Democrats don't let things like facts get in the way of a good narrative. After the ruling, Senator Chuck Schumer (D - N.Y.) said[33], "This decision is a body blow to what America stands for—equal access to the polls." Even after the Supreme Court ruled, the Left continued to push falsehoods to their constituents. There was a more measured response from Republicans. "This is only a burden for those who want to vote more than once," said[34] Brian C. Bosma, Indiana House Republican leader. "It protects everyone."

This Indiana case is not the only court case that addresses the topic of voter suppression. During every election cycle, we hear about alleged suppression taking place in North Carolina. The state is tarnished by allegations going all the way back to 2013, when Republican Governor Pat McCrory signed into law legislation requiring photo identification at the polls. The bill also shortened early voting from 17 days to 10. Although both measures were aimed at reducing the possibility of fraud, Democrats feigned outrage and (you guessed it) cried racism and voter suppression. Progressive advocacy organization *Think Progress* called it[35] "the most aggressive voter suppression law in the nation—possibly the most aggressive such law since Jim Crow" before casting an even wider net by calling any voter ID requirement at all "a common method of voter suppression." They also alleged—without evidence—that the motive of the North Carolina legislature was to eliminate the first week of early voting because African Americans disproportionately used the first week of early voting.

The Daily Beast reported[36], "The ban on early voting hit Democrats more than Republicans: In 2012, 48 percent of North Carolina's early voters were registered Democrats and 32 percent were registered Republicans, an edge of 140,000 Democratic voters." Yet, disparate impact is not a declaration of intent.

Just hours after Governor McCrory signed the law, the ACLU and several other organizations filed a lawsuit (that train's never late!) alleging that the actual goal was to suppress voter turnout among black people, the poor and the elderly. "It is a trampling on the blood, sweat and tears of the martyrs black and white who fought for voting rights in this country," the Reverend William Barber, president of the state chapter of the NAACP told the *Guardian*[37]. "It puts McCrory on the wrong side of history."

The case made its way to the U.S Court of Appeals for the 4th Circuit, which ruled that North Carolina "acted with almost surgical precision" in its supposed targeting of black voters. The court also said the law imposed "cures for problems that did not exist." Despite the fact that this ruling was issued[38] by a hard Left court, the ruling is axiomatically cited now by anyone looking to "prove" that Republicans try to suppress the black vote. *The Washington Post* noted[39] DNC Chairman Tom Perez as saying, "This is a huge victory for voters and a massive blow to Republicans trying to restrict access to the ballot, especially in communities of color." The only part of his statement that was actually honest was his use of the phrase "massive blow to Republicans." The 4th Circuit assumed motive and relied on supposition, stating the justifications for the law by Republicans "cannot and do not conceal the State's true motivation." Now seems like a good time to remind everyone that the 4th Circuit was referred to[40] as "the cutting edge of liberal activism."

The ruling by the 4th Circuit was not universally accepted as a fair and correct decision. As Hans A. von Spakovsky of the Heritage Foundation wrote[41]:

"The plaintiffs, in addition to failing to produce witnesses unable to vote because of these changes, produced no voter-turnout information to support their false claims. The actual turnout data show that voters were not kept out of the polls by any of these requirements.

"The Justice Department's so-called experts claimed that turnout would be depressed because—in a patronizingly

> *racist claim that the Fourth Circuit believed—black voters*
> *are 'less sophisticated' and can't figure out how to register*
> *and vote. But as the district court had already discovered,*
> *black voters in North Carolina actually 'fared better in*
> *terms of registration and turnout rates in 2014, after the*
> *new law was implemented, than in 2010, when the old*
> *provisions were in place.'*

> *"African-American turnout 'not only increased, but did so*
> *at a greater rate than that of other groups (including*
> *whites).' Yet the Fourth Circuit discounted this evidence."*

Despite attempts by North Carolina Republicans, the U.S. Supreme Court declined to hear the case to reinstate the voter ID law. But, NPR's Pam Fessler said[42], "Chief Justice John Roberts wrote that the court's refusal to consider an appeal did not signify an opinion on the merits of the case."

Despite the ruling by the 4th Circuit, a majority of Americans actually support identification measures to help ensure the integrity of our elections. A Pew Research study from 2012 showed[43] that 77 percent of Americans actually favor Photo ID Voting requirements. By 2016, that number had grown to 80 percent[44].

Considering so much attention is given to claims that mandating voter ID laws will disenfranchise minority voters, it is again interesting to note how minority voters actually feel on this issue. *The Weekly Standard* reported on a Gallup poll[45] in 2016 showing that "77 percent of American Hispanics and Blacks support voter ID laws."

It's a phenomenon that we see across the entire nation. A Quinnipiac Poll[46] shows big majorities of voters support "efforts to require voters to show a photo identification card to vote." In Florida, 77 percent support it; in Ohio, 75 percent support it; and in Pennsylvania, 64 percent support it. One poll found[47] that more than 72 percent of North Carolina residents supported voter ID laws. In Iowa, roughly 70 percent[48] of people support them.

The idea of requiring identification to vote is not anathema to regular everyday Americans who want to make sure their vote actually counts. Most people don't fall victim to claims that any attempt to verify someone's identity is a ploy to suppress their vote.

Of course, there are some legitimate examples of actual voter suppression, but the examples are fewer than examples of actual voter fraud. Avvo, a website that offers legal help, listed some[49] of the most egregious examples of what they consider to be real voter suppression. Some check out and some do not. Several examples are provided below:

1. In the 2008 election cycle, flyers were posted at Drexel University in Philadelphia, Pennsylvania stating that underground police were going to be on campus making arrests on Election Day. ABC News[50] reported, "The flyer reads like a friendly letter to fellow students relaying a warning from an 'Obama supporter': 'He informed me that on the day of the election there will be undercover officers to execute warrants on those who come

to vote based on the anticipated turnout,' writes the anonymous student in the letter ... 'He advised me if I had any outstanding warrants or traffic offenses I should clear them up prior to voting.'" This example qualifies as suppression because of the intent to scare people into staying home and not voting.

2. In the 1980s, Republican organizations created a Ballot Security Task Force (BSTF), which was to patrol certain urban precincts, warning residents that voter fraud could land them in prison. The signs carried by BSTF read: THIS AREA IS BEING PATROLLED BY THE NATIONAL BALLOT SECURITY TASK FORCE IT IS A CRIME TO FALSIFY A BALLOT OR TO VIOLATE ELECTION LAWS. *The New York Times* reported[51] that "the task force included off-duty police officers who carried weapons in plain sight." The task force challenged voters at the polls and even blocked the way of some voters. Although the Essex county Prosecutor, George Schneider, investigated and found only "technical" violations of state law (not suppression) and chose not to prosecute, a civil lawsuit was filed by the Democratic National Committee, alleging that the Republican National Committee has violated the Voting Rights Act by engaging in harassment and voter intimidation. The lawsuit was settled[52] in 1982 with a consent decree in lieu of a

trial, which said they would not repeat such tactics. It also required the RNC to allow a federal court to review any new ballot security initiatives.

3. In 2006, "Virginia voters received fake voicemail messages from the state elections commission stating that the voters were registered in other states and would be arrested if they tried to vote in Virginia." This tactic appears to have been repeated in 2017. The Prince William County NAACP posted on Facebook on November 6, 2017, asserting reports of voters receiving calls indicating that their polling place had changed. They somehow identified the calls as originating from Gloucester, VA and Adairsville, GA. In their post, they said[53], "It is vital that everyone knows these phone calls are fraudulent and are attempted voter suppression. We as an organization have fought for decades to have as many eligible people in our community participate in the electoral prcoess [sic] as possible; these attempts at voter suppression cannot succeed."

4. In 2008, the New Black Panther Party faced accusations of voter suppression after members showed up at a polling place brandishing billy clubs and intimidating people who weren't there to support then-candidate Obama. A civil complaint was filed, and Chairman Malik Shabazz was one of three members charged with violating the Voting Rights Act. One member was caught

on video referring to whites as "crackers" and was charged with brandishing a deadly weapon. It was reported[54] that "the Obama administration won a default judgment in federal court in April 2009 when the Black Panthers didn't appear in court to fight the charges. But the administration moved to dismiss the charges in May 2009." Former Justice Department official J. Christian Adams, who worked there during the Obama administration, quit over the handling of the case, saying his[55] former superiors instructed "attorneys in the civil rights division to ignore cases that involve black defendants and white victims."

5. Democratic activist Gigi Gaston documented more 2,000 complaints of suppression against the Obama campaign during the 2008 primaries. She stated that the DNC deprived American voters of their choice of Hillary Clinton as the nominee. *The Gateway Pundit* transcribed her television interview and reported[56], "Senator Clinton, by all accounts, except caucuses, won the Primary Election and, therefore, should be the 2008 Democratic Nominee. That didn't happen, due largely to illegitimate and illegal acts. We have interviews of many accounts from caucus states recounting threats, intimidation, lies, stolen documents, falsified documents, busing in voters in exchange for paying for "dinners," etc. There are at least 2000

complaints in Texas alone of irregularities directed towards the Obama Campaign that have led to a very fractured and broken Democratic Party." Gaston made a documentary entitled *We Will Not Be Silenced*, which featured "teachers, professors, civil rights activists, lawyers, janitors, physicists, ophthalmologists, accountants, mathematicians, [and] retirees" who discuss how Democrats have disenfranchised them through rampant fraud.

6. The State of Colorado came under fire when it purged names from its voter rolls within 90 days of the 2008 election. *The New York Times* said[57] that the purge appears to have been conducted in violation of federal law, but that the actions did not "seem to be coordinated by one party or the other." They also admitted that it was unlikely that officials intentionally broke the rules. States are only allowed to remove names from voter rolls within 90 days if the voter has died, moved out of state or been declared unfit to cast a vote. However, Colorado Secretary of State Mike Coffman said[58] that allegations of improprieties were "way off." A review of the data found 2,454 duplicate voter registrations cancelled and more than 14,000 other registrations cancelled within 90 days of the election. Coffman said, at the time, that his office was determining if that action was in violation of the law. *The Denver Post* reported[59]

that of the 14,049 voter registrations that were removed, "6,572 voters had moved out of the county or state, 4,434 registrations were listed as duplicates, 1,145 voters were deceased and the remainder was a mix of convicted felons, people with incomplete applications, those who were not U.S. citizens and withdrawn registration applications."

The idea of rampant voter suppression is alive because its proponents define it with such wide parameters as to include nearly any policy or piece of legislation with which they disagree. In the chapter on the 2018 midterms, we saw the story of a man in Georgia who claimed voter suppression, although the facts showed he simply failed to register on time. His inability to cast a ballot was his own fault. In many states, we hear allegations of voter suppression because states clean up their voter rolls by lawfully purging names. What's most striking, however, is that we so often hear cries of voter suppression to suppress policies that would increase transparency and accountability in our own elections. The question we should all be asking is: why? Who wins and who loses in a system where we are unable to verify people who are casting ballots? Who benefits from the loopholes that some work diligently to keep from closing? What advantage do some states have by keeping millions of names of ineligible voters registered? The answer at this point should be obvious.

You can tell who benefits from election fraud by simply

observing who fights tooth and nail against policies that would prevent it.

Elections are central to the proper functioning of our constitutional republic. Yet, a relatively small number of Americans fully trusts our election system. A Gallup poll[60] from 2016 revealed that only 30 percent of Americans felt confident in the "honesty of elections." Part of restoring confidence means taking more seriously the notion of verifying that only legal, legitimate voters are casting ballots in U.S. elections.

When we see data and hear stories of fraud or a system so vulnerable that the potential for fraud is highly likely, it erodes trust in the process of how we select our leaders.

Ironically, the lack of security in our elections—the feeling that one's vote might not matter—actually decreases turnout. In other words, *it* suppresses the vote.

CHAPTER 7

The Presidential Advisory Commission on Election Integrity

"Facts do not cease to exist because they
are ignored."

—*Aldous Huxley*

Throughout the years there have been multiple organizations involved, in some capacity, with election fraud. Some of those organizations were investigated for facilitating fraud, but one was recently created to determine the extent to which voter fraud might be taking place in the United States.

In May of 2017, President Trump convened the Presidential Advisory Commission on Election Integrity to study the issue of election fraud and how pervasive this type of fraud might be in the U.S. The commission was chaired by Vice President Mike Pence. Kansas Secretary of State Kris Kobach was the Vice Chair. Not surprisingly, this body was met with hostility. The *Washington Post* reported[1] that "Michael Waldman, president of the Brennan Center for Justice, called the commission 'a sham and distraction,' alleging that the announcement was an attempt by Trump 'to pivot' from his firing" of former FBI Director James B. Comey. People For the American Way dismissed the commission as a manifestation of President Trump's so-called inability to accept his supposed loss of the popular vote in 2016—a red herring, inimical to advancing the cause of voting rights.

Yet, as we've seen in earlier chapters, there are myriad examples of voter fraud that have been taking place chronically and in numbers great enough to swing presidential and congressional elections. This commission was hardly a ruse. Its creation was necessitated by specific examples of real fraud that have taken place throughout the country. President Trump called for an examination of the nation's elections after asserting that between 3 and 5 million illegal votes were cast against him in the 2016 election—a claim that we have already seen is likely to be true.

Kobach issued a letter to all 50 states requesting data, but states were not eager to cooperate. Much of the reason for resistance concerned privacy, as states were being asked to turn over information including names, addresses, dates of birth, last four digits of social security numbers, political party, felony convictions, military status and all sorts of other information that the commission said could ultimately become available to the public. The commission even asked state officials to transmit that sensitive data[2] via an unsecured website. Appalled at the wide scope of the information being requested, Connecticut Secretary of State Denise Merrill published the copy of the letter[3] that she received, which stated:

Dear Secretary Merrill,

I serve as the Vice Chair for the Presidential Advisory Commission on Election Integrity ("Commission"), which was formed pursuant to Executive Order 13799 of May 11, 2017. The Commission is charged with studying the registration and voting processes used in federal elections and submitting a report to the President of the United States that identifies laws, rules, policies, activities, strategies, and practices that enhance or undermine the American people's confidence in the integrity of federal elections processes.

As the Commission begins its work, I invite you to contribute your views and recommendations throughout this process. In particular:

1. What changes, if any, to federal election laws would you recommend to enhance the integrity of federal elections?

2. How can the Commission support state and local elec-

tion administrators with regard to information technology security and vulnerabilities?

3. What laws, policies, or other issues hinder your ability to ensure the integrity of elections you administer?

4. What evidence or information do you have regarding instances of voter fraud or registration fraud in your state?

5. What convictions for election-related crimes have occurred in your state since the November 2000 federal election?

6. What recommendations do you have for preventing voter intimidation or disenfranchisement?

7. What other issues do you believe the Commission should consider?

In addition, in order for the Commission to fully analyze vulnerabilities and issues related to voter registration and voting, I am requesting that you provide to the Commission the publicly available voter roll data for Connecticut, including, if publicly available under the laws of your state, the full first and last names of all registrants, middle names or initials if available, addresses, dates of birth, political party (if recorded in your state), last four digits of social security number if available, voter history (elections voted in) from 2006 onward, active/inactive status, cancelled status, information regarding any felony convictions, information regarding voter registration in another state, information regarding military status, and overseas citizen information.

You may submit your responses electronically to Election-IntegrityStaff@ovp.eop.gov or by utilizing the Safe Access File Exchange ("SAFE"), which is a secure FTP site the federal government uses for transferring large data files. You can access the SAFE site at https://safe.amrdec.army.mil/safe/Welcome.aspx. We would appreciate a response by July 14, 2017. Please be aware that any documents that are submitted to the full Commission will also be made available to the public. If you have any questions, please contact Commission staff at the same email address.

On behalf of my fellow commissioners, I also want to acknowledge your important leadership role in administering the elections within your state and the importance of state-level authority in our federalist system. It is crucial for the Commission to consider your input as it collects data and identifies areas of opportunity to increase the integrity of our election systems.

I look forward to hearing from you and working with you in the months ahead.

I'm not sure that anyone should be entirely comfortable with such sensitive information being aggregated and then put into the hands of a government body that fully intended to make it all public. Aside from ethical considerations, compliance with the commission's request would have been a violation of multiple states' laws. The *New York Times* reported that[4] "many states bar the release of even partial Social Security numbers or other personal information because that data can be used for identity theft." As of July 2017, the states that refused to participate[5] in the commission were: Arizona, California, Connecticut, Indiana, Iowa, Kansas, Kentucky, Massachusetts, Minnesota, Mississippi, Montana, New Mexico, Nevada, New York, North Carolina, North Dakota, Ohio, Oklahoma, Oregon, Pennsylvania, Rhode Island, South Dakota, Tennessee, Texas, Utah, Vermont, Virginia, Washington and Wisconsin.

While security concerns were a factor, much of the refusal to cooperate with the investigation seemed rooted in a desire to avoid transparency. And, as per usual, the easiest way for state officials and activists to shut down discussion into potential election meddling was to play the race card.

Vanita Gupta, the president of the Leadership Conference on Civil and Human Rights and former head of the Justice Department's Civil Rights Division, absurdly claimed[6] that the entire purpose of the voter commission was to legitimize voter suppression. It was on this basis that seven different lawsuits were filed in response to the commission's founding. Voter suppression and false claims of racism were used as weapons to obstruct justice and prevent—once again—a serious look into the existence and extent of voter fraud.

A lawsuit by the NAACP's Legal Defense fund stated that President Trump[7] "appointed a commission stacked with biased members to undertake an investigation into unfounded allegations of voter fraud," that the work of the commission is "grounded on the false premise that Black and Latino voters are more likely to perpetrate voter fraud," and that "the planned actions of the Commission evince an intention to discriminate against African-American and Latino voters." This line of reasoning completely ignores the fact that the commission was bi-partisan, not made up only of Republicans. But, there is no end to race-baiting when it comes to obstructing any attempts at an honest look at election fraud.

Reading the complaint in its entirety is a case study in delusion, by the lawsuit's reliance on assumptions, ignoring evidence that supports the creation of the commission (some of which you've already read about in this book), ascribing suspicious motives to individuals who have well-founded arguments and repeatedly playing the race card as a weapon to beat up opposition. This lawsuit was not about protecting minorities. The lawsuit was not about preventing communities from becoming disenfranchised. It was about one thing: shutting down the conversation through demagoguery. The fact that it took place within the framework of a legal filing is irrelevant. The goal and end result were the same.

"Now the important work of improving the integrity of the election process will be done by people who believe in election integrity, not by those who seek to preserve vulnerabilities in the system. Over the years, demonstrable and empirical data has been developed showing noncitizen voting, double voting, and defects in the election system that no credible observer could deny," The Election Law Center wrote[8], in a statement. "Some news outlets and activists have decided to ignore those facts, as if they do not exist. Unfortunately, there are plenty of well-funded groups, activist academics and individuals who are not credible who sought to undermine and sabotage the Commission's work."

When asked about assertions that the commission was really there to engage in voter suppression, commissioner and former Ohio Secretary of State Ken Blackwell said, "We push back and say this is a bipartisan commission. Bill Garndner, a fellow commissioner, and I have both been treasurer of our state and secretary of state. When we were treasurers, we wanted to make sure that we were out in front of our vulnerabilities and threats to protect the dollars of taxpayers in the state. Here, we want to make sure that we're protecting the integrity of the system, because we don't want anybody's legal ballot to be negated.

"Just think about how many elections—whether it's for tax levies, school tax levies, hospital levies, important local elections for office—are decided by one vote. We don't want the system corrupted by voters who are voting who shouldn't be voting and we want to make sure that we have cooperation across our states to protect the integrity of the system," he said. "It's a simple mission."

Yet, the lawsuit[9] painted a different picture entirely, accusing President Trump of using racially-coded statements and said, "Trump and his spokespersons and surrogates repeatedly used language that linked voter fraud to voters of color through targeted references to majority-minority cities and 'illegals' or 'illegal voters,' referring to immigrants." But, the "targeted references" simply pointed to instances where fraud took place. The skin color of the residents had nothing to do with it. And references to illegals are appropriate because they are not, in fact, "immigrants" if they have not immigrated here legally and have not become citizens. We shouldn't even have to parse such vitriolic, irresponsible language, but this is what you constantly get from people who would like nothing more than to prevent full transparency on this issue.

The Brookings Institute said[10], "The priorities of the bipartisan commission should be shifted from inconsequential allegations of voter fraud to acts of suppression that continue to historically and systematically disenfranchise African Americans and other vulnerable groups." But, illegal votes that cancel out legal votes (included under "legal votes" are votes cast by African Americans) is the definition of suppression. Brookings actually undercut its own argument against the role of the commission when it acknowledged: "There were reports in 2004 that 4,755 deceased voters[11] cast ballots in New Jersey. After careful comparison between voter rolls and death records, there were no official accounts of voter fraud. In New York in both 2002 and 2004, 2,600 deceased voters allegedly voted, only to be removed from the register after an investigation revealed clerical errors and not malfeasance." This type of close examination of data to prove or disprove allegations of fraud—to confirm or dismiss allegations of malfeasance—is exactly what the commission was tasked to do but on a national level. If voter fraud were to be conclusively dismissed as a fantasy, the way to go about making that determination would be a structure similar to (or exactly the same as) the one assembled by President Trump. Obviously, any evidence of voter suppression would fall under that mandate by default and be investigated as well.

It's not unreasonable to propose an organization aggregate information on patterns of fraud taking place in many regions around the country. An outside supervisory body of some sort is really the only means to sort this out in a way that is both transparent and credible. You'd be a fool to think that jurisdictions that tend to benefit from voter fraud would just wake up one day and self-correct.

Despite the resistance to President Trump's Commission on Election Integrity, the concept of a panel assembled at the presidential level to study election issues is not new. In 2013, President Obama announced his own commission to study election issues. The executive order establishing the commission said that it would[12] "ensure that all eligible voters have the opportunity to cast their ballots without undue delay, and to improve the experience of voters facing other obstacles in casting their ballots, such as members of the military, overseas voters, voters with disabilities, and voters with limited English proficiency."

The primary focus of the Obama election commission seemed to be finding ways to expand access to voting, while the primary goal of the Trump election commission seemed to be eliminating the potential for fraud.

It's difficult to credibly suggest that the president's intentions in creating the commission were in bad faith when considering all of the information that's already known about voter fraud. Conceptually, the Trump commission was well founded. But, it overreached in its request for sensitive information. Had it guaranteed the privacy of the personal data submitted from states, there might have been a different outcome. Instead, it was a huge missed opportunity to deliver a clearer picture of just how compromised the integrity and security of our elections might be.

Nevertheless, there was still plenty of room for cooperation in sharing information on the seven key questions that were raised in the letter. Without violating anyone's privacy, they could have recommended changes to election laws, provided advice on additional security measures, raised issues that prevent them from ensuring fair elections and provided information on fraud or registration issues. They should have provided information on election-related convictions, given advice on preventing voter intimidation and given any additional information that would have been able to be used to secure future elections in a way that minimized suppression and harm to voters.

Across the country, there is actually much evidence that our election systems are not secure and that fraud is taking place. Election fraud is not only limited to the voters themselves but can also include actions by state and local election officials, including secretaries of state and others within the election supply chain. With the ability of states to arbitrarily withhold information from scrutiny, it becomes difficult to learn definitively of the activities that are actually taking place in our elections. It is crucial that some sort of oversight body be created that has the power to conduct real, meaningful oversight of all 50 states to ensure their compliance with the law.

That this "investigation" was forced to end so abruptly is a sign that many people around the country simply have no interest in exposing the corruption within our election systems. I, however, am not one of those people.

CHAPTER 8

Google: Big Tech Leviathan Election Meddling

> "Power is in tearing human minds to pieces and putting them together again in new shapes of your own choosing."
>
> —*George Orwell,* 1984

On June 24th, 2019, corruption watchdog Project Veritas (PV) released a video that featured hidden camera footage of Jen Gennai, Google's Head of Responsible Innovation. This footage reveals the company's contempt for oversight as well as her openly admitting Google's intent to interfere in the 2020 election.

"Elizabeth Warren is saying we should break up Google. And like, I love her but she's very misguided, like that will not make it better it will make it worse, because all these smaller companies who don't have the same resources that we do will be charged with preventing the next Trump situation, it's like a small company cannot do that," she said[1].

Google, still incensed over the result of the 2016 presidential election, is exploring ways to tilt the next presidential election in a way that satisfies their own political leanings and social mores.

"We all got screwed over in 2016, again it wasn't just us, it was, the people got screwed over, the news media got screwed over, like, everybody got screwed over so we've rapidly been like, what happened there and how do we prevent it from happening again," Gennai said. "We're also training our algorithms, like, if 2016 happened again, would we have, would the outcome be different?"

Project Veritas founder James O'Keefe said, "This is the third tech insider who has bravely stepped forward to expose the secrets of Silicon Valley. These new documents, supported by undercover video, raise questions of Google's neutrality and the role they see themselves fulfilling in the 2020 elections."

The day the video was posted, O'Keefe wrote on Twitter[2] that they had received two privacy complaints from YouTube for the video, which exposed the Google executive saying they would "prevent the next Trump situation." Later that day, YouTube (a subsidiary of Google) deleted the video. Fortunately, people across the country had already downloaded it.

The problem with Google's political bias and desire to impede a U.S. election is that it is illegal, which is why PV sent a letter to Congress, formally informing them of their findings. The letter stated[3]:

"Google's plans to intervene in the 2020 electoral cycle implicate clear violations of federal election law. Under the Federal Election Campaign Act ("FECA"), federal election law prohibits corporations from making contributions. This prohibition includes in-kind contributions by corporations where something of value is offered that supports or opposes a candidate for office. As an incorporated entity, Google is forbidden under the FECA to use resources to 'never let somebody like Donald Trump [to] come to power again.' It is similarly forbidden to promote candidates it would favor. Using its massive resources to alter search results, impact electoral internet traffic, or otherwise attempt to prevent a candidate from winning an election are all illegal acts when done by corporate actors. The captured video of Ms. Gennai illustrates that Google is currently 'training [its] algorithms' and is thus taking concrete steps likely in violation of federal election law.

"The Federal Election Commission has no shortage of examples of past prohibited corporate contribution enforcement matters. 2 But these have usually occurred before the rise of the influence of big tech companies and social media platforms. Just as it would be illegal for a corporation to give free private jet transportation to favored candidates, but not to others, any use of corporate resources to advance or hinder candidates online is equally suspect and should

> *be evaluated. 3 This should be a grave concern for the*
> *Department of Justice and the Federal Election Commis-*
> *sion."*

Gennai wrote a blog post[4] accusing PV of selectively editing and splicing the video to distort her words and actions of her employer, despite the fact that most of the video was unedited and her comments were...well...her comments. She says in the blog post that "Project Veritas has edited the video to make it seem that I am a powerful executive who was confirming that Google is working to alter the 2020 election. On both counts, this is absolute, unadulterated nonsense, of course," and that "Google has no notion of political ideology in its rankings," but there is plenty of evidence that shows the company's bias is pervasive and has a rather long history.

Soon after the PV video was published, a Google employee leaked an email in which the company labeled prominent conservative speakers Ben Shapiro, Dennis Prager and Jordan Peterson as "nazis."

"...if we understand that PragerU, Jordan Peterson, Ben Shapiro et al are nazis using the dog whistles..." the email states[5]. "I don't think correctly identifying far-right content is beyond our capabilities. But if it is, why not go with Meredith's suggestion of disabling the suggestion feature?" None of the three are "far Right." To the contrary, two are Jewish and the other is fairly centrist, making assertions that any of them are Nazis not only irresponsible but laughable. Additionally, all of them despise and speak out against not only the alt Right but extremism in general. The fact that official action was taken by Google against them, based on this false premise and clear mislabeling, is clear evidence of bias.

More and more, we are seeing not only Google's political bias but the bias of multiple major tech companies as they ramp up attacks against people who are guilty of nothing more than not identifying as politically progressive.

For nearly three years, we've had near nonstop coverage of Russian interference in the 2016 presidential election after that nation ran a few thousand Facebook ads. The U.S. House Permanent Select Committee on Intelligence conducted its own investigation into the influence Russia may have exerted over the 2016 election. But, Russian influence over U.S. elections pales in comparison to the influence American tech companies exert. In their final report[6], the House intel committee said that "58% of the 11.4 million impressions associated with Russian Facebook advertising occurred after the election," that "99% of Russian Facebook ads were funded with less than $1,000," and that 25% of the ads were never even seen. If Russia is running such a low-budget effort—one that wasn't even effective-- with most of that effort happening after the election results were already in, and it warrants an investigation from a special counsel, then billion-dollar companies with a clear political bias, a paper trail of manipulation, and statements of their intent to actively work to prevent the election of a presidential candidate they don't like should certainly have the sustained attention of Congress and the U.S. Department of Justice. Because, by all accounts, Google is meddling in U.S. elections more than Russia did.

The influence Google could exert over an election was warned of back in 2015 by Robert Epstein, a senior research psychologist writing for *Politico*. The subtitle of the piece cuts straight to the chase, saying[7], "Google has the ability to drive millions of votes to a candidate with no one the wiser."

"Given that many elections are won by small margins, this gives Google the power, right now, to flip upwards of 25 percent of the national elections worldwide," Epstein wrote. "In the United States, half of our presidential elections have been won by margins under 7.6 percent, and the 2012 election was won by a margin of only 3.9 percent— well within Google's control."

Epstein cites a 2015 study he and Ronald Robertson conducted for the *Proceedings of the National Academy of Sciences* (PNAS), which conducted experiments with more than 4,500 people to determine the degree to which search engine results can exert influence. Dubbed the search engine manipulation effect (SEME), the study found that through manipulation of search engine rankings, the voting preferences of undecided voters can easily be shifted by 20% (up to 80% in some demographics). The findings were so conclusive that the researchers actually called search engine manipulation a serious threat to our system of government.

The report[8] concludes:

"Although voters are subjected to a wide variety of influ-

ences during political campaigns, we believe that the manipulation of search rankings might exert a disproportionately large influence over voters for four reasons:

"First, as we noted, the process by which search rankings affect voter preferences might interact synergistically with the process by which voter preferences affect search rankings, thus creating a sort of digital bandwagon effect that magnifies the potential impact of even minor search ranking manipulations.

"Second, campaign influence is usually explicit, but search ranking manipulations are not. Such manipulations are difficult to detect, and most people are relatively powerless when trying to resist sources of influence they cannot see (66–68). Of greater concern in the present context, when people are unaware they are being manipulated, they tend to believe they have adopted their new thinking voluntarily (69, 70).

"Third, candidates normally have equal access to voters, but this need not be the case with search engine manipulations. Because the majority of people in most democracies use a search engine provided by just one company, if that company chose to manipulate rankings to favor particular candidates or parties, opponents would have no way to counteract those manipulations. Perhaps worse still, if that company left election-related search rankings to market forces, the search algorithm itself might determine the *outcomes of many close elections.*

"Finally, with the attention of voters shifting rapidly toward the Internet and away from traditional sources of information (12, 61, 62), the potential impact of search engine rankings on voter preferences will inevitably grow over time, as will the influence of people who have the power to control such rankings.

"We conjecture, therefore, that unregulated election-related search rankings could pose a significant threat to the democratic system of government."

In 2018, a study[9] for the American Institute for Behavioral Research and technology was conducted by Epstein, along with Roger Mohr Jr. and Jeremy Martinez. The title was "The Search Suggestion Effect (SSE): How Search Suggestions Can Be Used to Shift Opinions and Voting Preferences Dramatically and Without People's Awareness." The findings of this study showed "that search suggestions can be used to create a win margin among undecided voters of nearly 80%." It also noted that "with personalized search suggestions, the effect will likely be even larger."

It also mentioned Google's bias in the 2016 election, noting that it was difficult to get Google's search engine to show any negative results for Hillary Clinton, despite the fact that negative search terms auto-populated in other search engines and dominated Google Trends. (More on this shortly.)

It's been demonstrated for years that there exists the real possibility for tech companies to exert enough influence over an election cycle to alter the outcome of the election itself. Biased search rankings are even more influential than bias in traditional media sources. Studies also show that roughly three-quarters of the participants demonstrated no awareness that manipulation was even taking place.

We know that Google, specifically, has been waging a war against its ideological opponents for years through its manipulation of search results. Most recently, in 2018, in a disgusting display of political bias, Google actually tweaked its search results to list[10] "Nazism" as an "official ideology of the California GOP." This is not the type of action a non-biased, open platform would take. Taking a look at the last presidential election cycle, we can see when the company began to ramp up its manipulation campaign.

Google's political interference is well-documented yet infrequently discussed outside of conservative circles. During the 2016 presidential campaign, Google manipulated[11] its search results to favor Hillary Clinton over Donald Trump, which isn't surprising considering Eric Schmidt, the executive chairman of Google's parent company, Alphabet, Inc., was working for the Clinton campaign, going so far in his activism that he created a brand new company intended to help her win the election. Leaked emails show[12] Schmidt consulting on a robust list of campaign-related issues.

In 2016, a video[13] from SourceFed News showed how Google used its auto-complete feature to boost favorable search results for Hillary Clinton, while also boosting unfavorable results for then-candidate Donald Trump. As *The Federalist's* Bre Payton wrote[14], "By typing 'Hillary Clinton cri' into Google's search bar, the top auto-complete results are 'Hillary Clinton crime reform,' 'Hillary Clinton crime reform 1994,' and 'Hillary Clinton crisis.'

By contrast, the top auto-complete options when searching for the same thing in Yahoo and Bing resulted in 'Hillary Clinton criminal charges,' 'Hillary Clinton crimes,' and 'Hillary Clinton criminal.'"

CNN dismissed[15] the video as a conspiracy theory, saying that the company's algorithm filters out inaccurate information from its autocomplete feature, so the fact that Clinton hadn't been formally indicted was the reason why the results for Clinton displayed what they displayed.

That Google altered its results does show an intent to manipulate what users saw, regardless of what the company's motive might have been. But, looking at all the facts surrounding this issue, as SourceFed's narrator said, "The intention is clear: Google is burying potential searches for terms that could've hurt Hillary Clinton in the primary elections over the past several months by manipulating recommendations on their site."

Epstein notes the two-fold tactics big tech use to manipulate politics, stating[16], "The technology guarantees the win, and the donation guarantees allegiance, which Google has certainly tapped in recent years with the Obama administration." Now, with executives admitting to wanting to stop President Trump from winning in 2020, there seems to be not only an influence operation running but an attempt to position the company as an uncontested kingmaker.

But, auto-complete tampering is not the only way Google manipulates the platform's users.

"**GOOGLE, INC., ISN'T** just the world's biggest purveyor of information; it is also the world's biggest censor," was the first line in a piece that ran[17] in *U.S. News & World Report* about Google blacklists that automatically filter out certain content. The report notes that algorithms that block access to information can also shift votes. Preempting the "but it's a private business that can block what it wants" crowd, it stated[18]: "If Google were just another mom-and-pop shop with a sign saying, 'we reserve the right to refuse service to anyone,' that would be one thing. But as the golden gateway to all knowledge, Google has rapidly become an essential in people's lives – nearly as essential as air or water. We don't let public utilities make arbitrary and secretive decisions about denying people services; we shouldn't let Google do so either."

The nine blacklists the company setup are:

1. The autocomplete blacklist
2. The Google Maps blacklist
3. The YouTube blacklist
4. The Google account blacklist
5. The Google News blacklist
6. The Google AdWords blacklist
7. The Google AdSense blacklist

8. The search engine blacklist

9. The quarantine list

The manipulation of search results based on your personal data (like search, browsing and purchase history) is known as a "filter bubble." Google's competitor, search engine DuckDuckGo, describes filter bubbles as pernicious when a user is searching political topics, because[19] "undecided and inquisitive voters turn to search engines to conduct basic research on candidates and issues in the critical time when they are forming their opinions on them. If they're getting information that is swayed to one side because of their personal filter bubbles, then this can have a significant effect[20] on political outcomes in aggregate." If you're not familiar, DuckDuckGo is a platform that was created to protect user privacy and provide unbiased results in its search engine. It doesn't track you, save user data or manipulate search results.

Back in 2012, DuckDuckGo conducted a study[21] showing that Google's filter bubble might have "significantly influenced the 2012 U.S. Presidential election by inserting tens of millions of more links for Obama than for Romney in the run-up to that election." The study used participants who entered identical search terms at the same time and found:

> *Most participants saw results unique to them. These discrepancies could not be explained by changes in location, time, by being logged in to Google, or by Google testing al-*

gorithm changes to a small subset of users.

On the first page of search results, Google included links for some participants that it did not include for others, even when logged out and in private browsing mode.

Results within the news and videos info-boxes also varied significantly. Even though people searched at the same time, people were shown different sources, even after accounting for location.

Private browsing mode and being logged out of Google offered very little filter bubble protection. These tactics simply do not provide the anonymity most people expect. In fact, it's simply not possible to use Google search and avoid its filter bubble.

It also found that some users saw suggestions for links that others didn't see; they were "offered domains seen by no-one else. If you were one of these people, you would have no way of knowing what you're missing," the report found. More disturbingly, it also found that Google is able to (and does) tailor your search results even if you're browsing in what you *think* is private mode.

The danger with Google's manipulation is that it has the ability to control people's perception of reality. It has the power to shape what individuals think about any topic or individual by showing you what it wants you to see when you're conducting research, and it does so without the user's awareness that it's happening. Their algorithms shaped the public's perception of America's last president, Barack Obama, and they've shaped the public's perception of our current president, Donald Trump. People don't always believe what *they* believe, they believe what companies like Google *want* them to believe. This manipulation could easily be considered a mass psy-op (psychological operation).

Not only have these types of algorithms contributed to the increased polarization in our country, they give the technology companies that deploy them the ability to quietly shape public policy and to help guide the outcome of elections. With this much power, it's easy to understand why comments about intentionally shaping the 2020 election would be taken very seriously. And, the expose by PV isn't the only recent example of people within Google showing political bias. In March 2019, a leaked recording[22] of Google's senior director of U.S. public policy, Adam Kovacevich, said he and a "majority of Googlers" wanted to "steer conservatives" away from nationalism and toward their version of a message of liberty and freedom. Additionally, back in 2016, a leaked email from Eliana Murillo, former head of Google's Multi-cultural Marketing department, showed that the company used its power to try and help the Clinton campaign. In a commentary on this issue Fox News's Tucker Carlson said[23]:

> *"In her email Murillo - Murillo touts Google's multi-faceted efforts to boost Hispanic turnout in the election. She knows that Latinos voted in record-breaking numbers*

especially in states like Florida, Nevada and Arizona, the last of which she describes as 'a key state for us.'

"She brags that the company used its power to ensure that millions of people saw certain hashtags and social media impressions with the goal of influencing their behavior during the election.

"Elsewhere in the email Murillo says 'Google supported partners like Voto Latino to pay for rides to the polls in key states.' She describes this assistance as 'a silent donation.'"

...

"In the end, Google was disappointed as Murillo herself conceded 'Ultimately after all was said and done, the Latino community did come out to vote and completely surprised us. We never anticipated that 29 percent of Latinos would vote for Trump. No one did. If you see a Latino Googler in the office please give them a smile. They are probably hurting right now. You can rest assured that the Latinos of these blue states need your thoughts and prayers for them and their families. I had planned a vacation and thought I would be taking the time to celebrate. Now, it will be time to reflect on how to continue to support my community through these difficult times.'

"Nobody at the DNC was more upset by the results than

Murillo. Google tried to get Hillary elected. They failed this time. We reached out to Google. The company did not deny that the email was real or that it showed a clear political preference. Their only defense was that the activities it described were either non-non-partisan or weren't taken officially by the company. But of course they were both.

"Plenty of people in Google knew what was going on and we've seen no evidence that anyone in Google disapproved of it or tried to rein it in. Two years later, Google is more powerful than it's ever been and the Left has increasingly become radical in what it is willing to do to regain political power.

"What could Google be doing this election cycle to support its preferred candidates? What could they do in 2020 is a question almost nobody in Washington seems interested in even asking. They ought to be interested."

And these aren't just staffers at the company who deeply lament Google doing even more to try and secure a political outcome of their own preference. Shortly after Clinton's embarrassing 2016 defeat, Google held a company-wide meeting. Video of the meeting was sent to *Breitbart News* by an anonymous source and displayed for the world to see the animus held by the company's top brass toward America's political right. *Breitbart's* Allum Bokhari wrote a piece breaking down key moments (along with an embedded, unedited video of the meeting, including):

Google co-founder Sergey Brin said that[24] he was "deeply offended by the election of Trump" and that the result of the election "conflicted with many of [Google's] values."

CFO Ruth Porat apparently broke down in tears before committing to more activism and manipulation, saying that the company would "use the great strength and resources and reach we have to continue to advance really important values."

Brin also praised the suggestion of an audience member to increase "matched Google employee donations to progressive groups" before disparaging Trump voters by calling them extremists and saying support for the president could be attributed to income disparity.

The company's executives burst into laughter when asked if they saw anything positive from the election's outcome.

Based on this sort of conduct, along with numerous allegations that not only Google but its subsidiary, YouTube, was biased against conservatives, one could expect a congressional hearing on the matter. In 2019, Epstein did testify before Congress about his findings. This was pursuant to separate hearings that were held in December 2018. While the hearing covered multiple topics, it did include questions about allegations that Google censored or manipulated its platform against conservatives. Rep. Zoe Lofgren (D-CA) asked[25]: "Now, manipulation of search results. I think it's important to talk about how search works. Right now, if you Google the word 'idiot' under images, a picture of

Donald Trump comes up. I just did that. How would that happen? How does search work so that that would occur?" After a short exchange, Pichai stated, "We don't intervene on any particular search result." What's problematic is, that statement is simply not true.

Just a few days after Google's congressional hearing, a writer for Slate was searching the term "abortion" on YouTube and was unhappy with the results. She emailed YouTube complaining that anti-abortion videos dominated the search results. Then, just a few days later, after she searched again, all of the results were different. According to former Google engineer Mike Wacker, writing for *Medium*, a spokesperson for YouTube[26] "stressed that the company is working to provide more credible news content from its search and discovery algorithms," meaning that the company does manually intervene in search results—the exact opposite of what Pichai said in his congressional testimony. Additionally, a memo about Google's blacklists was sent to[27] *The Daily Caller*, which confirmed a "manual component" to the company's blacklisting process. It was also reported[28] that the company manually intervened with "search terms related to: the Irish abortion referendum, Democratic Congresswoman Maxine Waters, and anti-gun activist David Hogg."

President Trump weighed in on Google putting its thumb on the scale, writing on Twitter[29]:

> *"Google search results for "Trump News" shows only the viewing/reporting of Fake News Media. In other words,*

they have it RIGGED, for me & others, so that almost all stories & news is BAD. Fake CNN is prominent. Republican/Conservative & Fair Media is shut out. Illegal? 96% of........results on "Trump News" are from National Left-Wing Media, very dangerous. Google & others are suppressing voices of Conservatives and hiding information and news that is good. They are controlling what we can & cannot see. This is a very serious situation-will be addressed!"

To anyone paying attention, it should be rather obvious that the president wasn't being hyperbolic. Why should he think any differently considering what we already have learned, including findings of a report by *The Wall Street Journal* in 2017 that showed Google employees[30] were considering ways to manipulate search functions help thwart President Trump's temporary travel ban?

This chapter only examines Google, not any other major tech companies and their ability to influence politics and elections. However, through the actions of Google and statements by its senior-level officials, we also see that big tech clearly has the will to do so as well.

CHAPTER 9

Electronic Voting Systems

"The tipping point for e-voting fraud, I
think, will be when they realize it's cheaper to
hire hackers than to buy campaign ads."

—Matt Blaze

Exercising one's right to vote is considered a sacred right in
the United States, but it has not always been a right held by
everyone equally in our country. Until 1870, when the 15th
amendment to the Constitution was passed, which prohibited states from denying the right to vote based on "race,
color, or previous condition of servitude[1]," only white men
could vote. Women were granted the right to vote in 1920
after the 19th amendment was passed[2]. In 1924, Native
Americans were granted citizenship after the passage of the
Indian Citizenship Act, and by 1948 all states withdrew
prohibitions on Indian voting[3]. In 1965, the Voting Rights

Act eliminated poll taxes and other structural barriers that targeted minorities[4].

Fast forward to 2019, and much of the conversation is no longer about systemic impediments to voting (though some pretend such encumbrances still exist) but about figuring out ways to increase voter turnout.

In the last few election cycles, only about 60 percent of the eligible voting population showed up in presidential elections as did roughly 40 percent during midterm elections[5]. So, conversations about how to increase participation should be expected.

Many believe that an expansion of technology could boost voter turnout, helping more people exercise their right to vote. From newer versions of electronic voting machines at the polls to internet voting and even mobile apps, ideas for electronic voting are plentiful. And so are the opportunities to compromise those systems.

A 2018 report from the National Academies of Sciences, Engineering and Medicines[6] warned about the vulnerabilities in electronic voting systems and advised they not be used in the United States. "To protect the integrity and security of U.S. elections, all local, state, and federal elections should be conducted using human-readable paper ballots by the 2020 presidential election," the report says[7]. "In addition, every effort should be made to use paper ballots in the 2018 federal election. Ballots that have been marked by voters should not be returned over the Internet or any network connected to it, because no current technology can guarantee their secrecy, security, and verifiability."

The Academy's study on U.S. voting systems was conducted for two years. A press release from the Academy said that the committee that conducted the study "included computer science and cybersecurity experts, legal and election scholars, social scientists, and election officials." Additionally, the report warned that the risks associated with electronic and internet voting are "more significant than the benefits.[8]"

The report outlined multiple steps that federal, state and local governments needed to take to improve infrastructure and better defend the integrity of their elections.

Regarding internet and mobile voting, one of the Academy's key recommendations[9] is that "Internet voting should not be used at the present time, and it should not be used in the future until and unless very robust guarantees of secrecy, security, and verifiability are developed and in place. Currently, no known technology can guarantee the secrecy, security, and verifiability of a marked ballot transmitted over the Internet."

In like manner, they also suggested that "elections should be conducted with human-readable paper ballots. Paper ballots form a body of evidence that is not subject to manipulation by faulty software or hardware and that can be used to audit and verify the results of an election."

Technology has improved the lives of Americans in countless ways. Most automobiles have dozens of computers managing everything from traction control and air conditioning to seat cooling. Advances in computing have reduced the size of a personal computer from a 2,000-pound, refrigerator-size IBM 305 RAMAC[10] to a hand-held iPhone with the ability to record high-definition video in 4K. Advances in 3D printing now allow a person to print furniture, clothing, utensils, cars, games and even body parts[11]. Yet, as far as we've come, we still have a long way to go to develop the kind of electronic architecture needed to guarantee the security and integrity of our elections.

MOBILE/SMARTPHONE VOTING

A Pew Research Center study showed that, as of 2017, roughly 77 percent of Americans owned a smartphone. With such a high market penetration and the easy availability of new apps, it would be only natural for some to suggest that our nation begins the transition to mobile voting applications. Voting by phone sounds like a feasible idea to some, but it presents significant hurdles that would need to be overcome prior to becoming an accepted form of voting.

"There are so many things that could go wrong," Marian Schneider, president of Verified Voting, a coalition of computer scientists and government transparency advocates pushing for more-secure elections, told the *Los Angeles Times*[12]. "It is an odd time for this to be gaining momentum."

There are a number of startups that are pushing the use of blockchain technology as a means to secure mobile voting systems. But, as the non-partisan, non-profit election security organization Verified Voting says[13], "Vendors of online election software, with a vested interest in selling their products, of course downplay the inherent risks and promise the oxymoronic 'Internet security.'"

The *LA Times* report said that many of the proponents of vote-by-phone technology say that using blockchain technology would provide adequate layers of security, stating that blockchain "leverages a network of potentially thousands of independent computers with their own security systems, aiming to diffuse risk. Promoters of such voting say hackers could not alter an election without penetrating thousands of independent security systems.[14]"

However, it also issued a warning from cryptographers who said that a vote-by-phone app could indeed be breached and designed to rig votes and that "blockchains themselves introduce new security vulnerabilities."

The report outlined potential vulnerabilities in such a system, using a description of a pilot mobile voting program undertaken by West Virginia officials. The steps and vulnerabilities are listed as follows:

1. **Application**. This is where a "voter emails a mobile voting form to the county clerk."
2. **Authorization**. In this step, "the county clerk approves the request and the voter is then invited to participate in mobile voting."
3. **Authentication**. This is where the voter "downloads the app and completes the identification verification process." ***Potential security gap***: a) "the app could be hacked remotely, hacked by a bad ac-

tor embedded at the app company" or b) "malware on the phone infects the app."

4. **Voting**. "The voter receives, marks, verifies and submits a ballot that is biometrically secure (using fingerprint or facial recognition). ***Potential security gap***: "Biometric technology fails, infected or compromised app changes the vote."

5. **Transmission**. "Votes are encrypted, transmitted, verified and immutably secured. ***Potential security gap***: "Verification software gets corrupted, cloud systems housing blockchain may be a potential entry point for hackers."

6. **Voter verification**. The voter is emailed a digitally signed receipt and the secretary of state gets an anonymous ballot receipt. ***Potential security gap***: "The system keeps track of how each voter voted, creating a risk of decryption and breach of confidentiality."

The front-end is not the only place in the digital supply chain where votes could be compromised. Once the tabulation process begins, there still exists the potential for fraud.

7. **Preparation**. "Before the election, the county clerk and a staff member enroll for credentials."

8. **Tabulation**. "The county clerk and another election official open the digital ballot box and print and tabulate ballots."

9. **Postelection audits**. "The canvass board com-

pares the ballot receipts with the full ballots. ***Potential security gap***: "Paper ballot is vulnerable to alteration by corrupted software."

While mobile voting may seem convenient, it introduces new security challenges. A mobile voting platform could possibly increase turnout, but it certainly would create new and plentiful opportunities for fraud to take place. Voting means nothing if your vote is discarded or cancelled out by an illegal vote—we must prioritize security over convenience.

"When it comes to U.S. elections, the current attack surface is vast enough," Tom Kellermann, chief cybersecurity officer at security company Carbon Black told *The Daily Swig*[15]. "There is no need to create additional exposure and risk by adding smartphones into the equation. Before looking to make elections easier, let's first make them more secure by adding a mandatory paper trail."

In general, there seems to be widespread concern among cybersecurity professionals over the prospect of electronic and internet voting.

Venafi, a global cybersecurity firm, conducted a study that concluded[16] that "93% of security professionals are concerned about cyber-attacks targeting election infrastructure and data." It also found that only two percent of security professionals felt confident in federal, state and local governments' ability to detect cyber-attacks that target election infrastructure. If vulnerabilities are so pervasive on hardware and software tightly controlled by federal, state and local governments, there is no reason to believe there would be fewer vulnerabilities existing on the average person's cell phone. It's rather surprising to see states like West Virginia testing out mobile voting in a real-world scenario with actual votes being cast.

In 2018, *Wired* reported that West Virginia military personnel would be the guinea pigs for mobile voting[17]. Security experts lamented the fact that no one, to this day, has been able to demonstrate the ability to secure a mobile voting platform. "From what is available publicly about this app, it's no different from sending voting materials over the internet," Marian Schneider, president of the nonpartisan advocacy group Verified Voting told[18] *Wired*. "So that means that all the built-in vulnerability of doing the voting transactions over the internet is present." The report cites a study by Consumer Reports, showing that 33 percent of respondents would be more likely to vote if they were able to do it from a mobile or internet-based platform. But, that desire doesn't mitigate the security risks: malware, spoofed links redirecting the voter to a different website, viruses and denial of service attacks.

"There is wide agreement among computer security experts that this is problematic," David Dill, a professor emeritus in computer science at Stanford, told[19] the *LA Times*. "It disturbs me that officials are getting enthusiastic about this voting technology without talking to the people who have the expertise to evaluate its security." For the foreseeable future, mobile voting carries far more risks than benefits, and it doesn't produce a paper trail to verify the accuracy of the votes that are cast.

Assurances by tech startups asserting they somehow have "cracked the code" are more of a sales pitch to get states to buy their software rather than a guarantee that their systems are immune from tampering.

In March 2019, Switzerland discovered a critical flaw in the election system used by the Swiss government, which allowed valid votes to be changed into[20] "nonsense that would not be counted," according to a paper published by researchers. Additionally, there may not even be a way to determine who was responsible without compromising the privacy of all voters in the election.

Cyberscoop reported that this study was published just a week after it was learned that the Swiss government's electronic voting system "could enable outsiders to replace legitimate votes with fraudulent ones.[21]" The article quoted Sarah Jamie Lewis, executive director of the Open Privacy Research Society, who decried the platform's use in national elections because of a "critical cryptographic vulnerability," despite the fact that the code used was hailed as "state-of-the-art."

Myriad examples from around the globe attest to the fact that we are still a long way from having electronic voting platforms to which the public can assign a great deal of confidence.

VOTING MACHINES

Security challenges related to electronic voting are not new. After all, at polling places across the country, many jurisdictions have had some form of electronic voting system for years. These are known as Direct Recording Electronic (DRE) Systems. Verified Voting describes these systems22 as using interfaces, such as a pushbutton, touchscreen or dial, to record votes directly into the device's computer memory. The votes are stored in some type of memory cartridge. Some of the DREs are equipped with a Verified Voter Paper Audit Trail (VVPAT), which prints a voter's selection and allows them to verify their selections with an independent paper trail prior to the vote being recorded on the memory device.

As of November 2018, states that used a DRE system with a paper trail included[23]: Alaska, Arizona, Arkansas, California, Hawaii, Idaho, Illinois, Missouri, Nevada, North Carolina, Ohio, Washington D.C., West Virginia, Wisconsin and Wyoming.

States that used a DRE system without a paper trail included[24]: Florida, Indiana, Kansas, Kentucky, Louisiana, Mississippi, New Jersey, Oklahoma, Pennsylvania, South Carolina, Tennessee, Texas and Utah.

Other states still use paper ballots.

All in all, about 70 percent of states use some type of electronic voting system, and for years, we have seen evidence that those systems can be hacked or manipulated to change votes.

In 2016, *CBS News* reported on just how vulnerable U.S. systems are to fraud. Brian Varner, a researcher at Symantec Security Response, showed how—with just a few dollars—anyone can hack a voting machine. Anyone is able to buy a special card that can slide into a port on a standard voting machine. "For $15 and in-depth knowledge of the card, you could have the vote," he said[25]. Varner was able to vote, then insert the card into the machine, which reset the machine and allowed him to vote again. This process can be repeated, allowing anyone with this device the ability to cast an untold number of votes for any candidate of their choosing.

The report also cited Symantec director Kevin Haley, who said that elections can also be hacked after votes have been cast at a machine. "The results go from that machine into a piece of electronics that takes it to the central counting place," Haley told CBS. "That data is not encrypted and that's vulnerable for manipulation." Just as we've seen with mobile and internet voting systems, he affirmed that even with electronic voting machines there are "many places in the voting process once it goes electronic that's vulnerable" to hacking.

In addition to hacking threats, there are other potential vulnerabilities when these systems are deployed. In 2018, just months prior to the midterm elections, *Newsweek* reported[26] that Election Systems and Software, one of the country's largest voting machine makers, admitted that it preinstalled software on voting machines that allowed it remote access. While the system isn't used to cast ballots, it *is* used to tabulate official results and program voting machines[27]. Shortly after this disturbing information became public, Senator Ron Wyden (D-Or) wrote on Twitter[28], "Installing remote-access software and modems on election equipment is the WORST decision for security short of leaving ballot boxes on a Moscow street corner. Congress MUST pass my bill to require paper ballots and audits."

In August 2018, Las Vegas hosted DefCon, a 25-year-old hacking conference, where thousands of hackers from around the world met at Caesars Palace and demonstrated to the world just how easy it is to hack voting machines used in U.S. elections. The election system portion of the conference took place in the "Voting Village," one of more than ten areas where attendees could learn about and practice hacking techniques. Having participants use actual voting machines and replicas of state government websites was meant to be a demonstration of the potential vulnerabilities of these systems in real-world applications. The event's organizers went to great lengths to try to find machines that are currently in use. "There's been a lot of claims that our election system is unhackable. That's BS," said Jake Braun[29], one of the village's organizers, in an interview with *Fortune Magazine*. "Only a fool or liar would try to claim that their database or machine was unhackable."

The New Yorker ran a piece on the event and profiled an eleven-year-old girl who was able to successfully hack into a replica of the Florida Secretary of State's election website. "First, you open the site," she said[30] to the magazine, "then you type a few lines of code into the search bar, and you can delete things and change votes. I deleted Trump. I deleted every single vote for him." Sue Halpern, writing for *The New Yorker*, said that the day of the event the National Association of Secretaries of State issued a statement suggesting the hacking done at the conference's "pseudo environment" would not necessarily translate to success in a real-world scenario. Halpern also interviewed Braun to get his thoughts on the press release. "It's totally tone-deaf," he told her. "A nation-state is literally hacking our democracy—wouldn't you want to take any help you could possibly get? If they don't think that the Russians are not doing what we're doing here all year, as opposed to just a weekend, then they are fucking idiots, right?"

Although hacking into a state's election site in real life would not necessarily allow an intruder to change any votes, as Halpern notes, you don't have to change vote count to manipulate an election. Should a hacker be able to access voter registration data, they could sabotage the data to prevent someone from being able to cast a ballot when they show up to vote. "Change a letter in the spelling of a voter's name, change a house number, strike someone from the registry altogether, and when they show up at the polls they're going to be turned away," she wrote. "This is crucial: votes don't need to be changed and voting machines don't need to be tampered with for an election to be hacked."

But, are there any other examples of voting machines actually being hacked? During the 2018 midterm elections in Texas, there were multiple reports of electronic machines changing votes: both Democrats whose ballots indicated an erroneous votes for Republican Ted Cruz and Republicans whose ballots showed[31] erroneous votes for Democrat Beto O'Rourke. However, state officials determined that the issue occurred when voters turned the dial to select a candidate and hit the "enter" button at the same time—or when the interface was touched while the page was still loading[32]. There was no fraud or machine tampering involved.

But, back in 2009, five people in Kentucky were indicted in a scheme that involved election officials buying votes and instructing people on how to change votes on voting machines during three separate elections[33]. The machines were provided by ES&S.

In 2014, in North Carolina, several voting machines were taken out of service after it was reported that they were registering votes for a Republican Senate candidate, when the Democratic candidate was being selected. "I called one of the poll workers over," Percy Bostick told[34] *News & Record*. "She said do it again. And again, I touched the screen at the proper place for Kay Hagan, and it again reported it for Thom Tillis."

That same year in Illinois, it was reported that voting machines were changing votes from Republican candidates to Democrats. "I tried to cast a vote for myself and instead it cast the vote for my opponent," Jim Moynihan said[35]. "You could imagine my surprise as the same thing happened with a number of races when I tried to vote for a Republican and the machine registered a vote for a Democrat." Although the error was dismissed as a calibration error, Katie Pavlich, writing for *Townhall*, raised interesting questions: "This machine error was visible, what about the changes these machines are making to votes cast for Republicans that aren't visible? How many registered voters have had their votes and participation in the process stolen as a result of 'faulty' machines[36]?" Similar calibration issues were reported in South Carolina[37] in the 2018 midterm elections, with the machine selecting candidates above or below the candidate voters were attempting to choose.

In Pennsylvania, in the 2016 election, voters reported that machines were changing votes from then-candidate Trump to Hillary Clinton. "I went back, pressed Trump again. Three times I did this, so then I called one of the women that were working the polls over," Bobbie Lee Hawranko told[38] Pittsburgh's *CBS News* affiliate. "And she said you must be doing it wrong. She did it three times and it defaulted to Hillary every time." The issues with those systems were also brushed off as a calibration error.

Yet, despite the lengthy list of issues reported on these systems, these systems comprise 90 percent of the equipment used in U.S. elections. In March of 2019, a group of Senators called on" election equipment makers ES&S, Dominion Voting, and Hart InterCivic to explain why they continue to sell decades-old machines, which the senators say contain security flaws that could undermine the results of elections if exploited," wrote[39] Zack Whittaker writing for *TechCrunch*.

There was also a bipartisan bill introduced in 2019 called the *Secure Elections Act* "to strengthen election cybersecurity in America and protect against foreign interference in future elections.[40]"

Cyber Scoop reported that[41] the bill included "a provision for grant money originally allocated to states to be funneled to local jurisdictions. The bill directs the Election Assistance Commission to dole out grants to election offices that receive 'cyber hygiene' scans and vulnerability assessments from DHS. Other grants would fund organizations that replace electronic voting machines with ones that produce a paper trail. Election agencies can also receive reimbursements for conducting statistical risk-limiting audits by hand after an election."

Voting systems without paper trails can be easily compromised. Any legislation aimed at fortifying election systems should include some sort of paper ballot verification mechanism.

"One of the purposes of a postelection audit is to be able to detect and correct for the possibility that the computers have been hacked," Andrew Appel, a Princeton University computer science professor told the *Star Tribune*[42]. "What you audit are a bunch of electronic files that computers gave you. ... They can give you false files."

Georgia is one of a handful of states that uses completely electronic voting machines. In 2019, Georgia state lawmakers pushed legislation that would upgrade the state's 17-year-old DRE devices to a new voting system that would include a paper ballot: a measure agreed upon by both Democrats and Republicans. The goal is to have the system in place prior to the 2020 primary elections. Georgia State Senator Elena Parent (D) told[43] the *Atlanta Journal Constitution*, "We still need the people of Georgia to believe in the process, and right now they are unconvinced." The new system would be a hybrid between electronic voting machines, where voters would make their selections on a screen, and a paper ballot that would print after they've confirmed their selections. This would give voters an opportunity to review selections before inserting the ballot in an optical scanner. An additional benefit is that this system would create a digital record, as well as a paper record that could be compared post-election in an audit to determine the accuracy of the results.

Our elections are only as good as the confidence we have in them. It is possible for an architect to design a building so that the physical structure actually moves. This is done to mitigate the effects of natural phenomena like earthquakes. Our technology is so good that it's possible to have a building sway so much that people can feel it. However, even though the building itself might be completely secure, the people in it would not be psychologically secure in a building they feel moving. Likewise, the integrity of our elections is only as good as we *believe* it is. In order to maintain confidence in our government, we must be able to have a high degree of confidence in the system that is used to choose the leaders of our government. Updating our voting machines is a critical component in that equation.

CHAPTER 10

"Russian Collusion" and the Investigation of Special Counsel Robert Mueller

There was no collusion.

CHAPTER 11

What Does Election Fraud Have in Common with Alcoholism?

"It isn't that they can't see the solution. It is that they can't see the problem."

—*Gilbert K. Chesterton*

Dealing with election fraud in America is similar to dealing with an alcohol or drug addiction—the first step on the road to recovery is admitting you have a problem. And America has a big problem. Much like an addict has people around them who prod, scream, intervene and otherwise try anything to alert them to the fact that they have a serious problem and are engaging in destructive behavior, so too does our country have people trying to warn us of the very real problem of election fraud.

Just as an addict might be in denial—shunning any and all attempts to point out an issue that is visible to so many—until there comes a point of acceptance, there can never really be resolution.

We have to accept that there are certain truths, despite our political predilections, and be willing to work on a bipartisan basis to resolve our issues. Currently, if you ask those on the political Left if election fraud exists, you're likely to get a carefully crafted response telling you that there is "no evidence of *widespread* voter fraud." If you ask those on the Right, you'll probably get the simple answer of "yes." We need to bridge the gap.

It is crystal clear that illegal voting is taking place in the United States. Election fraud is real. It is rampant. This book outlines plenty of examples. It is also clear that our election apparatus remains vulnerable to fraud, some of which is incredibly difficult (if not impossible) to catch. For these reasons, we can only have low to moderate confidence in the overall security of our elections. A reassessment is needed, and changes need to be made to ensure that our election infrastructure is working as well as we are told it is.

In this final chapter, some of the challenges we need to face are addressed, along with a few suggestions for what needs to occur to patch up the holes in our broken election system.

PUBLIC AWARENESS OF THE TRUTH ABOUT ELECTION FRAUD

As it stands, the public does not get an accurate picture of the full scope of fraud and the potential for fraud in our elections. We have political operatives on video *admitting* to bussing people from polling location to polling location, state to state to vote illegally. They further admit they've been doing it for decades. And the mainstream media issued a blackout. We have Leftist activist groups filing lawsuits and accusing Republicans of being racists for pushing election security laws while their own members were getting *convicted* of voter fraud for voting up to ten times in a single election. I've outlined a considerable about of information showing the corruption taking place in this country. Yet, John Q. Public rarely, if ever, hears about it. Watchdog groups like Judicial Watch and Project Veritas have done a better job of exposing election fraud and informing the public than have legacy media, local governments and the U.S. Department of Justice. Greater efforts must be made to make the public aware of the sobering truths about voter fraud in the American electoral system. A major roadblock to facilitating real discussion is that when serious people are attempting to have a grownup conversation about this issue, many simply hurl epithets (i.e., "racism" and "voter suppression") to stifle dialogue, despite there being plenty of legitimate reasons why this conversation is needed. Calls to make our elections safer should result in real policy discussions, not false, divisive, salacious accusations.

Overall, people are unaware that the country has millions more registered voters than eligible voters. They don't understand how something as seemingly innocuous as inaccurate voter rolls can open the door to fraud. Many think that fraud in small numbers won't impact an election, because they fail to understand that many elections (including presidential elections) are decided by relatively small margins.

Additionally, people often see voter fraud as an act that can only be committed by people casting multiple or fake ballots, without the framework to understand that political operatives, elected officials and election workers themselves can (and do) engage in actions that illegally determine the outcome of an election. And, don't forget that many illegal aliens vote without *knowing* that it's actually illegal.

It doesn't take much to swing an election through corruption. Tech companies are censoring social media platforms because they have power and have displaced traditional media as the sole arbiters of truth. It's a highly effective way to share content legacy media won't touch. The public needs to take a lead role in sharing this information, not rely on the media to better understand this issue, demand more oversight and accountability and exercise a higher level of vigilance, not simply buy the lie coming across their television that there is "no evidence of widespread voter fraud."

THINK LOCALLY

In this current political climate, most people's attention is focused on politics at a national level. However, relatively few policies set in motion by D.C. politicians affect our lives on a daily basis. We've become so accustomed to focusing on Washington that we've lost sight of the fact that the decisions that impact us the most happen right around the corner. Congressional representatives aren't the ones making decisions about your child's school. Senators aren't creating election laws in your jurisdiction.

If we are to induce meaningful change, it's imperative to focus attention on electing local officials who are committed to enacting real election security. Local officials decide what machines are used and whether or not to vote online. They create directives and guidelines on chain-of-custody issues, regulate poll workers and more. Only vote for elections supervisors, secretaries of state, county recorders and officials who take election security as seriously as they do election participation. You can also get involved and become part of the process yourself. You can work as a poll watcher or take on another role in your city to help ensure that elections are being run fairly and in accordance with the law.

REQUIRE ID TO VOTE NATIONALLY

Instituting a national voter ID policy should be a prerequisite for casting a ballot—any ballot. It shouldn't have to be said, but this is one of the simplest measures to undertake to help secure American elections. States and local jurisdictions can (and should) still run their elections the way they choose, but verifying the identity of the person casting a vote should be compulsory. We should expect pushback against such a policy to be considerable, given that many people benefit from election fraud and prefer the system to continue operating as is. But, most of the exposure to corruption that we currently have originates from an inability to properly authenticate each and every ballot.

U.S. elections are a joke compared to other countries. As stated in Chapter 6, even Mexico has a national voter ID card that is required to vote in their country. It's not racist or an exercise in systematic disenfranchisement to adopt a similar system in ours.

If we are to be serious about election security, it is imperative that each jurisdiction verifies that the person casting the ballot is who they say they are and that they are a legal U.S. citizen—which is more difficult, now that multiple states such as California and Illinois automatically issue driver's licenses and alternative forms of identification to non-citizens.

It's worth reiterating that voter ID laws do not have a suppressive effect on turnout and are in no way racially targeted. In states that instituted voter ID laws, turnout (particularly among minorities) has been shown to have increased in many cases. Requiring identification to vote only disenfranchises those who are already ineligible to vote.

For those making the argument that obtaining an acceptable form of ID is too burdensome, please consider the following: There is a movement in the U.S. (particularly among 2020 presidential hopefuls) for payment of reparations to African Americans. Underpinning this idea is the notion that blacks can prove that they are descended from slaves. However, the very people suggesting that blacks can produce generations worth of papers and documents to prove they are descendants of slaves are the same people who suggest that blacks can't even figure out how to get an ID to vote. It's laughable. Further, it's patronizing and demeaning that black people are used as political pawns in this way.

America's constitutional philosophy on elections is "one person, one vote." There is no better way to guarantee this than to verify the identity of every single person casting every single ballot.

END BALLOT HARVESTING AND REFORM THE PROCESS FOR MAIL-IN AND ABSENTEE BALLOTS

Across multiple states, we have seen innumerable examples where ballot harvesting has resulted in fraud or created enough uncertainty about election results that the practice should be banned. No state or county in the U.S. should allow political operatives to collect individual ballots and return them; certainly not *en masse*. The only people who should even be considered to be allowed to turn in a ballot for a voter are a family member or someone who is actually living in their household.

In both North Carolina and California, ballot harvesting has created more problems than it has solved. It has diminished the confidence that any of us can have in the sanctity and security of our vote. Debate over the frequency with which such swindling might take place is irrelevant, because if it happens even once, it happens too much. We have an easy way to guarantee that this is never an issue: stop accepting harvested ballots.

We can have little confidence in a box of ballots that's just found in the back of someone's car, then dropped off at an election center to be tallied. All we have to do is recall the testimony of the political consultant from Texas who admitted that, in some cases, people (literally) sit around filling out thousands of blank ballots and turn them in to be counted. We can remember the video of the election commissioner in New York who said that he had no idea where *thousands* of absentee ballots even came from. They're just turned in and processed. Senior citizens and people for whom English is a second language are now being targeted in campaigns designed to steal their votes. People are on record voting multiple times and voting in the name of the deceased. This is an insane level of corruption.

Protections must remain for members of the U.S. military who are physically unable to vote, those with disabilities and those who have a sincere need to vote by mail or for an absentee ballot. But, considering the amount of fraud taking place via this system, it needs to be revised.

THE ELECTORAL COLLEGE

While it wasn't covered in the book, the electoral college is certainly worth a mention. The founders of our constitutional republic designed our governmental system with checks and balances. The executive, legislative and judicial co-equal branches of government disburse power and limit any one branch from becoming too powerful. Concerning elections, we have something similar: the electoral college.

Mob rule is as much a threat to sovereignty as is dictatorial governance, which is exactly why America has the electoral college. It gives equal representation to each state so that large masses of people congregated in small areas cannot run roughshod over the rest of the country. Crowded cities like New York and Los Angeles don't get to take away the rights of a rural town in Montana. To further put it into perspective—popular vote aside—in 2016 President Trump won 30 out of the 50 states and 2,623 counties to Hillary Clinton's winning of only 489 counties[1]. If we remove California from the mix and count just the other 49 states, President Trump beat Clinton by 1.2 million votes[2]. If we look at vote tallies without both California and New York, he beat her by three million votes[3]. *Most* of the country supported President Trump in the election.

The framers of the constitution were smart enough to create a system that did not rely on a simple majority vote to determine who is president. There is a growing movement by the progressive Left in America to abolish the electoral college. Since they believe this system cost them elections in 2000 and 2016, they now just want to burn it all to the ground. If this effort succeeds, the capricious whims of mob rule will trample the rights of those in the minority.

ELECTRONIC VOTING

Innovation occurs faster than the laws meant to regulate it. But, if we want to be able to have a high degree of certainly over the results of our elections, states and local jurisdictions must very carefully assess the types and pervasiveness of technological assets within their election architecture. Some components, such as the ability to audit results, should be mandatory. Why bother voting if it's just a crapshoot on whether or not your vote counts?

There are many new and emerging technologies that will make voting easier, but they must also make voting more secure. Sacrificing security for convenience should be a nonstarter for any official with a role in elections administration.

Concerning an electronic voting system, I fully support the ten rules for voting systems, as put forward by the Verified Voting Foundation[4]:

1. *It should use human-readable marks on paper as the official record of voter preferences and as the official medium to store votes.*

2. *It should be usable by all voters; accessible to all voters, in-*

*cluding those with disabilities; and available in all mandated
languages.*

3. *It should provide voters the means and opportunity to verify
that the human-readable marks correctly represent their intended selections, before casting the ballot.*

4. *It should preserve vote anonymity: it should not be possible to
link any voter to his or her selections, when the system is used
appropriately.*

5. *It should export contest results in a standard, open, machine-
readable format.*

6. *It should be easily and transparently auditable at the ballot
level. It should:*

> *export a cast vote record (CVR) for every ballot,
> in a standard, open, machine-readable format,
> in a way that the original paper ballot corresponding to
> any CVR can be quickly and unambiguously identified,
> and vice versa.*

7. *It should use commercial off-the-shelf (COTS) hardware
components and open-source software (OSS) in preference to
proprietary hardware and proprietary software, especially
when doing so will reduce costs, facilitate maintenance and
customization, facilitate replacing failed or obsolete equipment, improve security or reliability, or facilitate adopting*

technological improvements quickly and affordably.

8. *It should be able to create CVRs from ballots designed for currently deployed systems and it should be readily configurable to create CVRs for new ballot designs.*

9. *It should be sufficiently open to allow a competitive market for support, including configuration, maintenance, integration, and customization.*

10. *It should be usable by election officials: they should be able to configure, operate, and maintain the system; create ballots, tabulate votes, and audit the accuracy of the results without relying on external expertise or labor, even in small jurisdictions with limited staff.*

Additionally, until such time as they can be fully secured, all states should consider a moratorium on mobile and internet voting platforms. They are simply not secure, even with blockchain. We've seen and heard from technology experts in detail about how advances such as blockchain do not guarantee safe elections. Blockchain-based voting systems still have multiple vulnerabilities throughout the entire digital supply chain that can easily allow for unauthorized intrusions.

REGULARLY PURGE VOTER ROLLS

Voter rolls should be purged like diapers—and for the exact same reason. Much of the uncertainty about fraudulent voting is tied to the fact that we have millions more names on our voter rolls than we do living and eligible voters. As long as this remains the case, it will be impossible to guarantee that legal votes are not being cancelled out by illegal votes. Inaccurate voter rolls are the precursor for fraud with ballot harvesting, mail-in ballots, absentee ballots, people voting multiple times, buses driving people to multiple locations to vote, etc. A system where there is only one registration per one voter should be a goal on which we can all agree.

Opponents of voter purges assert that they disenfranchise lawfully registered voters when those voters' names are mislabeled as ineligible. Such cases are relatively rare, however. Additionally, voters can (and should) easily visit the website for their county prior to an election in order to confirm their registration.

What we do know is that many of the types of fraud and suspected fraud we've seen would be all but impossible if there weren't illegitimate names listed on voter rolls.

Purging voter rolls is consistent with the NVRA, but—and more importantly—it is consistent with helping to eliminate the potential for fraud. No system will ever be foolproof—after all, we do have to account for the fallibility of human beings. But we can certainly mitigate potential fraud with basic steps to ensure that only legal, eligible voters are even on voter rolls in the first place.

CROSSCHECK & ERIC

While the Crosscheck system—which checks voter information against information from other states to identify those registered in more than one state—isn't perfect, it has succeeded in identifying tens of thousands of people who are registered to vote in more than one state. As we've seen, there are people who have been caught voting multiple times, in multiple states. Having a system like Crosscheck in place where states routinely verify duplicate registrations is an obvious way to prevent such fraud from taking place.

Rather than dismiss the system outright because of a handful of false positives, Crosscheck should be tuned and then expanded so that any state is able to check the records of any of the other 49 states to determine if someone is registered to vote in more than one place.

A viable alternative to Crosscheck is the Electronic Registration Information Center (ERIC), which also identifies duplicate registrations and inaccurate voter roll data, but it does so with added security and in a more cost-effective manner. ERIC is a data center managed by Pew Charitable Trusts and participating states. It compares data from states' voter registration lists to data from the DMV, U.S. Postal Service, Social Security Administration and additional lists[5]. ERIC compares data from multiple sources simultaneously so states can know when someone on their voter rolls has passed away or moved out of state. This allows the state the person moved from to reach out and confirm the move and remove their name from their voter registration list; it also and allows the state the person moved to the opportunity to ask them to register to vote.

The ERIC system also anonymizes and encrypts sensitive information, like dates of birth, driver's license numbers and the last four digits of a voter's social security number. It offers "efficient and effective data matching" and "will result in such efficiencies as less returned mail, fewer provisional ballots on election day, shorter lines at polling places.[6]"

As of December 2018, there were 20 participating states, along with Washington D.C. And, since its creation, ERIC has resulted in more than 7.9 million in-state updates to voter registration lists. If your state is not participating, you should pressure your local government officials and elections supervisors for your state to become a member.

REINSTITUTE THE PRESIDENTIAL ADVISORY COMMISSION ON ELECTION INTEGRITY

If we are to get to the bottom of the issue of election fraud, there should be a formally assembled body that has the ability to thoroughly investigate all of the matters surrounding the potential for fraud in our elections. This wasn't even a contentious issue until President Trump took office. The Obama administration's election commission was largely praised, while the Trump administration's commission was derided from the moment it was announced.

Each state plays by its own rules. And when there is

enough evidence (circumstantial or otherwise) to warrant an investigation into potential corruption, if state attorneys general are unwilling to conduct those investigations, it's not unreasonable to suggest a broader review take place.

We have records of convictions, video evidence, affidavits, circumstantial evidence and a mountain of other data that show election fraud is real is happening and needs to be taken more seriously. Each state has control over its own election laws, so no federally assembled body has the statutory authority to compel specific policies. However, if an independent body can draw conclusions as to the facts about documented fraud and the risk for additional election fraud, a case that the public would support could be made for changes in how states and local jurisdictions run their elections.

Final Thoughts

Remember: You can always tell who is serious about stopping election fraud by observing which people fight tooth-and-nail against any measure that would prevent it. Free and fair elections are the lifeblood of our republic. They are what separate us from banana republics and repressive systems of subjugation. They allow the voice of the people to be exalted above the evil of tyranny. They must be protected, or we will cease to have true representative government.

We have the ability to create a system that would all but preclude election fraud. But, to build that system, we must have a better understanding of the ways in which our election system can be exploited. We also have to stop allowing our minds to be exploited, falling victim to emotional predators who try to convince us that this problem isn't real, despite the fact that we're able to see much of it.

Voting is a constitutional right and a civic duty in our country. Therefore, we should be able to have confidence that those who choose to exercise their right to vote actually have their vote counted. It's indisputable that voter fraud is taking place across the United States. It is also clear that because of vulnerabilities within our election apparatus, massive amounts of additional fraud could be taking place, completely undetected. We have examples of individuals knowingly committing voter fraud by casting multiple ballots. We have examples of people unwittingly committing voter fraud. There are examples of states intentionally weakening their laws, which has the effect of introducing the potential for more fraud, not less. We have millions more people registered to vote than we have eligible voters. This book has covered countless examples of flaws within our election system and this work is hardly comprehensive. America certainly has the *means* to correct these flaws. The only question is: do we have the *will?*

End Notes

INTRO

1. https://www.abc15.com/news/region-phoenix-metro/central-phoenix/kyrsten-sinema-takes-slight-lead-in-senate-race-over-martha-mcsally
2. https://www.heritage.org/election-integrity/report/where-theres-smoke-theres-fire-100000-stolen-votes-chicago
3. http://www.electionlawcenter.com/uncategorized/statement-on-presidential-advisory-commission-on-election-integrity/

CHAPTER 1

1. http://www.illegalaliencrimereport.com/uncategorized/mexican-national-caught-illegally-voting-five-times-in-texas/
2. https://www.joetaxpayer.com/26-surprising-facts-about-speeding-tickets/
3. https://www.nbcnews.com/politics/politics-news/texas-woman-gets-5-years-prison-voting-illegally-n861516
4. http://www.rasmussenreports.com/public_content/politics/general_politics/may_2015/most_democrats_think_illegal_immigrants_should_vote
5. http://www.rasmussenreports.com/public_content/politics/general_politics/may_2015/most_democrats_think_illegal_immigrants_should_vote

6. https://www.prnewswire.com/news-releases/house-rightfully-condemns-illegal-voting-but-refuses-to-fund-border-wall-says-fair-300719887.html

7. https://www.stephenleary.com/2018/09/one-republican-and-140-democrats-refuse.html

8. https://www.congress.gov/bill/115th-congress/house-resolution/1071

9. https://www.washingtontimes.com/news/2018/jul/26/noncitizen-voting-push-liberal-jurisdictions-draws/

10. https://www.washingtontimes.com/news/2019/mar/8/house-votes-favor-illegal-immigrant-voting/

11. ibid

12. ibid

13. https://www.youtube.com/watch?v=rCldQRaPXwo

14. https://newspunch.com/democrat-activists-illegals-vote/

15. https://www.wnd.com/2016/11/obama-encourages-illegal-aliens-to-vote/

16. http://nymag.com/intelligencer/2016/12/why-people-believe-obama-encouraged-illegals-to-vote.html

17. https://dailycaller.com/2018/01/08/leaked-memo-dreamers-are-critical-to-dems-future-electoral-success/

18. https://www.investors.com/politics/editorials/rasmussen-poll-on-illegals-voting-reveals-political-motivation/

19. https://www.theepochtimes.com/eliseo-medina-revolution-through-illegal-immigration_2748588.html

20. https://www.justfacts.com/immigration.asp#electoral

21. https://twitter.com/realDonaldTrump/status/802972944532209664

22. http://time.com/4582868/donald-trump-people-illegally-voted-election/

23. https://www.nytimes.com/2017/01/23/us/politics/donald-trump-congress-democrats.html

24. http://www.capoliticalreview.com/capoliticalnewsandviews/poll-13-of-illegal-aliens-admit-they-vote-2015-report/

25. https://www.breitbart.com/politics/2015/08/18/30-million-illegal-immigrants-in-us-says-mexicos-former-ambassador/

26. https://www.prweb.com/releases/minutemen/illegali mmigration/prweb418456.htm

27. https://nationaleconomicseditorial.com/2018/01/19/ yale-study-shows-23-million-illegal-immigrants/

28. https://insights.som.yale.edu/insights/yale-study-finds-twice-as-many-undocumented-immigrants-as-previous-estimates

29. https://yaledailynews.com/blog/2018/10/09/som-study-estimates-higher-undocumented-immigration-numbers/

30. https://www.washingtontimes.com/news/2017/jun/1 9/noncitizen-illegal-vote-number-higher-than-estimat/

31. https://www.politico.com/magazine/story/2015/10/il legal-immigrants-could-elect-hillary-clinton-213216

32. https://www.washingtonpost.com/nation/2018/11/16 /lou-dobbs-casually-makes-up-story-that-many-illegal-immigrants-voted-midterms-had-immense-impact/?utm_term=.7b4c985f17da

33. https://www.washingtonpost.com/news/the-intersect/wp/2016/06/16/six-in-10-of-you-will-share-this-link-without-reading-it-according-to-a-new-and-depressing-study/?utm_term=.9609d021cf2e

34. https://freebeacon.com/politics/dem-candidate-abrams-blue-wave-comprised-documented-undocumented/

35. https://freebeacon.com/politics/abrams-dont-need-conservative-values-win-georgia/

36. https://www.youtube.com/watch?v=2hjmKBfrycQ

37. https://townhall.com/tipsheet/guybenson/2014/03/1 9/fraud-local-nbc-investigation-discovers-dozens-of-illegal-voters-in-florida-n1811547

38. https://pjmedia.com/trending/2017/09/11/study-finds-non-citizens-unknowingly-registered-vote/

39. ibid

40. https://savejersey.com/2018/07/illegal-immigration-voting-san-francisco-new-jersey/

41. http://www.ncsl.org/research/immigration/states-offering-driver-s-licenses-to-immigrants.aspx

42. https://www.chicagotribune.com/news/local/politics/ct-met-rahm-emanuel-municipal-id-vote-20180216-story.html

43. https://www.chicagotribune.com/suburbs/lake-county-news-sun/crime/ct-lns-lake-election-charges-st-0312-20180311-story.html

44. https://www.foxnews.com/politics/ny-county-clerk-drivers-license-illegals-voter-fraud-dangerous

45. https://publicinterestlegal.org/files/Report_Alien-Invasion-in-Virginia.pdf

46. https://www.washingtontimes.com/news/2016/oct/17/no-voter-fraud-isnt-myth-10-cases-where-its-all-to/

47. https://www.washingtonpost.com/news/the-fix/wp/2014/10/27/does-my-state-require-identification-to-vote/?utm_term=.c0e469b84844

48. https://www.whiteoutpress.com/dems-show-illegal-immigrants-which-states-they-can-vote/

49. https://www.nbcnews.com/politics/immigration/san-francisco-allows-undocumented-immigrants-vote-school-elections-n893221

50. https://www.foxnews.com/us/california-to-auto-register-drivers-to-vote-sparking-fraud-concerns

51. https://www.dailysignal.com/2019/03/12/california-audits-dmv-for-100000-voter-registratio

52. https://www.latimes.com/politics/la-pol-ca-dmv-voter-registration-error-20180905-story.html

53. https://thehill.com/homenews/house/153079-gop-says-5000-non-citizens-voting-in-colorado-a-wake-up-call-for-states

54. https://www.denverpost.com/2017/07/11/colorado-voters-unregister-donald-trump-integrity-commission/

55. http://www.dailycamera.com/guest-opinions/ci_31123750/hillary-hall-request-unsettling-but-voter-data-needs

56. https://davidharrisjr.com/politics/100000-illegal-aliens-registered-to-vote-in-pennsylvania-spurs-lawsuit/

57. Ibid

58. https://www.politico.com/2016-election/results/map/president/pennsylvania/

59. https://onenewsnow.com/politics-govt/2019/02/07/pa-admits-thousands-illegally-registered-to-vote-in-state

60. https://www.alipac.us/f12/pennsylvania-sends-thousands-illegal-immigrants-non-citizens-voter-registratio-339105/

61. https://twitter.com/KenPaxtonTX/status/108889859 5653386240?ref_src=twsrc%5Etfw%7Ctwcamp%5Etweete mbed%7Ctwterm%5E1088898595653386240&ref_url=htt ps%3A%2F%2Fwelovetrump.com%2F2019%2F01%2F29 %2Fvoter-fraud-judicial-watch-estimates-900000-illegal-votes-were-cast-in-2018-midterms%2F

62. https://www.nytimes.com/2019/01/25/us/noncitizen s-voting-texas.html

63. https://www.politico.com/election-results/2018/texas/

CHAPTER 2

1. https://www.breitbart.com/video/2016/12/11/trump -im-not-taking-a-wrecking-ball-to-obamas-legacy-im-doing-whats-right/

2. https://www.huffingtonpost.com/entry/the-trump-doctrine-erasing-the-black-mans-legacy_us_5931705ee4b0649fff211835

3. https://www.breitbart.com/politics/2018/03/31/turle y-sessions-using-utah-federal-prosecutor-much-better-trump-2nd-special-counsel/

4. http://thefederalist.com/2018/11/10/palm-beach-county-democrats-argue-count-votes-cast-non-citizens/

5. http://www.leg.state.fl.us/Statutes/index.cfm?App_mo de=Display_Statute&Search_String=&URL=0100-0199/0102/Sections/0102.141.html

6. https://www.theepochtimes.com/florida-governor-rick-scott-sues-over-delayed-ballot-updates_2712176.html

7. https://www.breitbart.com/politics/2018/11/13/five-famous-examples-of-democrat-recount-boondoggles/

8. https://media.fox13news.com/media.fox13news.com/document_dev/2018/11/08/scottvsbucher_6365953_ver1.0.pdf

9. https://townhall.com/tipsheet/mattvespa/2018/11/09/fl-sen-palm-beach-county-election-supervisor-says-gop-lawsuit-could-be-racist-o-n2535697

10. https://cbs12.com/news/local/allegations-of-voter-fraud-in-deadlocked-council-race

11. http://postoncourts.blog.palmbeachpost.com/2016/04/21/voter-fraud-lawsuit-adds-intrigue-to-snakebit-riviera-election/

12. https://www.politico.com/magazine/story/2018/11/13/broward-county-florida-recount-222543

13. http://www.fox13news.com/news/florida-news/governor-rick-scott-warns-of-rampant-fraud-possible-in-broward-palm-beach-counties

14. https://twitter.com/marcorubio/status/1060609799719714817

15. https://media.fox13news.com/media.fox13news.com/document_dev/2018/11/08/scottvsnipes_6365954_ver1.0.pdf

16. https://www.breitbart.com/politics/2018/11/13/brenda-snipes-defiant-broward-recount-deadline-looms/

17. https://www.breitbart.com/politics/2018/11/16/broward-county-erases-gop-vote-gains-missed-recount-deadline-by-2-minutes/

18. ibid

19. https://www.nbcmiami.com/news/local/Broward-County-Uploaded-Recount-Results-2-Minutes-Late-500637162.html

20. https://townhall.com/tipsheet/mattvespa/2018/11/09/fl-sen-the-sordid-and-possibly-criminal-history-of-broward-countys-election-sup-n2535630

21. http://mediatrackers.org/2014/04/30/broward-county-creates-phantom-district-to-allow-illegal-voting/

22. https://www.nbcmiami.com/news/local/Broward-Countys-Election-History-at-the-Helm-of-Brenda-Snipes-500187112.html

23. https://dailycaller.com/2018/11/09/broward-florida-election/

24. https://www.sun-sentinel.com/local/broward/fl-sb-broward-elections-supervisor-broke-law-snipes-canova-20180514-story.html

25. https://www.miamiherald.com/news/local/community/broward/article221207380.html

26. https://www.miamiherald.com/news/politics-government/article3563324.html

27. https://www.miamiherald.com/news/local/community/broward/article220841135.html

28. https://www.miamiherald.com/news/local/community/broward/article109574732.html

29. https://www.sun-sentinel.com/news/fl-vote-by-mail-absentee-ballots-20140712-story.html

30. https://www.browardbeat.com/challenger-charges-broward-election-boss-brenda-snipes-ethically-challenged/

31. https://www.miamiherald.com/news/local/community/broward/article220841135.html

32. https://www.heritage.org/election-integrity/commentary/election-fraud-nonpartisan-issue-these-cases-florida-prove-it

33. https://www.miamiherald.com/news/local/community/broward/article220841135.html

34. https://thecapitolist.com/broward-recount-shenanigans-over-38000-democrat-votes-found-since-election-day-with-more-to-come/

35. https://www.politico.com/states/florida/story/2018/08/13/judge-sides-with-florida-gop-in-absentee-ballot-dispute-with-broward-county-555553

36. https://www.cbsnews.com/...

37. https://www.foxnews.com/politics/judge-sides-with-floridas-rick-scott-cites-violation-of-state-constitution-by-election-officials

38. https://www.foxnews.com/politics/judge-sides-with-floridas-rick-scott-cites-violation-of-state-constitution-by-election-officials

39. https://www.politico.com/states/florida/story/2018/11/14/federal-prosecutors-reviewing-altered-election-documents-tied-to-florida-democrats-695299

40. https://www.thegatewaypundit.com/2018/11/federal-prosecutors-discover-altered-election-documents-in-broward-county-tied-to-florida-democrats/

41. https://www.usatoday.com/story/news/politics/elections/2018/11/10/georgia-governor-race-stacey-abrams-pushed-concede-brian-kemp/1959470002/

42. https://www.theatlantic.com/politics/archive/2018/11/stacey-abrams-new-georgia-might-have-to-wait/575158/

43. https://thehill.com/homenews/campaign/417292-georgia-certifies-elections-results-in-bitterly-fought-governors-race

44. http://www.therepublic.com/2018/11/08/us-election-2018-georgia-provisional-ballots/

45. https://www.bloomberg.com/news/articles/2018-11-09/georgia-spike-in-temporary-ballots-signals-tampering-group-says

46. https://www.opednews.com/articles/Purged-Voters--Provisiona-by-Greg-Palast-Georgia-Election_Georgia-Politics_Rally_Voter-Rolls-Purged-181106-459.html

47. http://sos.ga.gov/index.php/elections/elections_and_voter_registration_calendars

48. https://www.newyorker.com/tech/annals-of-technology/how-voting-machine-lobbyists-undermine-the-democratic-process

49. https://www.wsbtv.com/news/state-politics/abrams-sues-for-more-time-kemp-s-campaign-says-math-is-clear/871570980?fbclid=IwAR3ijlf3ZwVGcQMgsJQ1oUBupFQEY1iUNjlA9UJpBXQq6iDG0Vv35ty6xEo

50. https://politics.myajc.com/news/state--regional-govt--politics/democrats-search-for-votes-before-georgia-election-results-finalized/yNspgifhm1NsnCXxVQRjiN/

51. https://twitter.com/CBSThisMorning/status/1163431
818185588736?ref_src=twsrc%5Etfw%7Ctwcamp%5Etwe
etem-
bed%7Ctwterm%5E1163431818185588736&ref_url=https
%3A%2F%2Flegalinsurrection.com%2F2019%2F08%2Fst
acey-abrams-says-conceding-the-georgia-gubernatorial-
race-would-make-her-complicit-in-an-unfair-system%2F
52. https://twitter.com/GOPChairwoman/status/116316
1928786685952?ref_src=twsrc%5Etfw%7Ctwcamp%5Etw
eetem-
bed%7Ctwterm%5E1163161928786685952&ref_url=https
%3A%2F%2Flegalinsurrection.com%2F2019%2F08%2Fst
acey-abrams-says-conceding-the-georgia-gubernatorial-
race-would-make-her-complicit-in-an-unfair-system%2F
53. https://freebeacon.com/politics/sherrod-brown-goes-
off-if-stacey-abrams-doesnt-win-in-georgia-they-stole-it/
54. https://dailycaller.com/2018/11/29/stacey-abrams-
voter-suppression-lawsuit-
cospon-
sor/?fbclid=IwAR1yPv1x8_dtPfPHW311YZpHgI7VPk5X
PHd0w6Ol1kQprAFqxmG7bFcou3c
55. https://politics.myajc.com/blog/politics/georgia-2018-
abrams-owes-50k-irs/etNFk22AxvDt8KsXpGaaaK/
56. https://www.cbs46.com/news/members-of-new-black-
panther-party-seen-holding-guns-stacey/article_26a9ee9a-
e0e5-11e8-80f3-db8cefa9eefc.html
57. https://www.usatoday.com/story/news/politics/electio
ns/2018/11/13/midterms-kyrsten-sinema-democrats-red-
state-purple/1976116002/
58. https://www.lifezette.com/2018/09/arizona-gov-taps-
jon-kyl-as-mccain-senate-replacement/
59. https://www.npr.org/2019/01/02/681208228/trumps
-judicial-appointments-were-confirmed-at-historic-pace-in-
2018
60. https://www.salon.com/2017/01/19/at-least-one-
democratic-congressman-is-already-preparing-to-impeach-
donald-trump_partner/

61. https://en.wikipedia.org/wiki/2018_United_States_Se nate_election_in_Arizona

62. https://freebeacon.com/politics/arizona-gop-announces-independent-audit-maricopa-county-recorder/

63. http://worldpopulationreview.com/us-counties/

64. https://www.vox.com/2018/11/8/18075478/midterm -elections-arizona-vote-count-mcsally-sinema

65. https://www.nbcnews.com/politics/elections/arizona-gop-sues-limit-mail-ballots-senate-race-n933866

66. https://www.scribd.com/document/432278236/Arizo na-Republican-Party-Election-Audit-2019

67. https://www.azleg.gov/FormatDocument.asp?inDoc= /ars/16/00549.htm&Title=16&DocType=ARS

68. https://www.azleg.gov/FormatDocument.asp?inDoc= /ars/16/00549.htm&Title=16&DocType=ARS

69. https://docs.google.com/spreadsheets/d/1mAAOhwE T4GJW6RY6kBtuMPaG99muiiPnYUKbNIif3Gs/edit#gi d=0

70. https://www.nass.org/sites/default/files/surveys/2017 -10/state-laws-polling-place-electioneering-2016.pdf

CHAPTER 3

1. https://www.investors.com/politics/editorials/u-s-has-3-5-million-more-registered-voters-than-live-adults-a-red-flag-for-electoral-fraud/

2. https://www.nationalreview.com/2017/08/election-fraud-registered-voters-outnumber-eligible-voters-462-counties/

3. https://www.investors.com/politics/editorials/u-s-has-3-5-million-more-registered-voters-than-live-adults-a-red-flag-for-electoral-fraud/

4. http://www.latimes.com/politics/essential/la-pol-sac-essential-politics-updates-there-are-now-more-registered-voters-in-1475694802-htmlstory.html

5. https://www.nationalreview.com/2017/08/election-fraud-registered-voters-outnumber-eligible-voters-462-counties/

6. http://www.judicialwatch.org/press-room/press-releases/judicial-watch-warns-california-clean-voter-registration-lists-face-federal-lawsuit/

7. https://www.westernjournal.com/dick-morris-ghost-voters-keep-democrats-in-office/

8. http://nypost.com/2017/07/14/the-vote-fraud-that-democrats-refuse-to-see/

9. http://www.nationalreview.com/article/303062/neces sary-hygiene-deroy-murdock

10. http://www.miamiherald.com/2012/06/12/2845111/floridas-voter-purge-sparks-lawsuits.html

11. https://foreignpolicy.com/2012/11/06/foreign-election-officials-amazed-by-trust-based-u-s-voting-system-2/

12. https://www.breitbart.com/midterm-election/2018/08/15/exclusive-eric-eggers-nearly-250-counties-have-more-registered-voters-than-eligible-voters/

13. https://publicinterestlegal.org/blog/scores-of-counties-put-on-notice-about-corrupted-voter-rolls/

14. https://publicinterestlegal.org/blog/scores-of-counties-put-on-notice-about-corrupted-voter-rolls/

15. http://citizensnews.blogspot.com/2018/10/who-benefits-from-ghost-voters-well.html

16. https://losangeles.cbslocal.com/2016/05/23/cbs2-investigation-uncovers-votes-being-cast-from-grave-year-after-year/

17. https://www.westernjournal.com/new-investigation-discovers-voting-fraud-in-southern-california/

18. https://www.pewtrusts.org/~/media/legacy/uploaded files/pcs_assets/2012/pewupgradingvoterregistrationpdf.p df

19. https://chicago.cbslocal.com/2016/10/27/2-investigators-chicago-voters-cast-ballots-from-beyond-the-grave/

20. https://www.westernjournal.com/new-investigation-discovers-voting-fraud-in-southern-california/

21. https://www.dnainfo.com/chicago/20161019/downto wn/vote-rigged-elections-history-fraud-stolen-trump/

22. http://www.startribune.com/ballot-applications-from-dead-voters-found-in-alaska-race/491850091/

23. https://denver.cbslocal.com/2016/09/22/cbs4-investigation-finds-dead-voters-casting-ballots-in-colorado/

24. https://townhall.com/tipsheet/guybenson/2014/04/03/oh-my-evidence-of-massive-voter-fraud-in-north-carolina-n1818137

25. http://www.newser.com/story/153331/30k-dead-voters-registered-in-nc-but.html

26. https://www.charlotteobserver.com/news/local/crime/article146938034.html

27. http://www.therepublic.com/2018/01/09/01092018cr_dead_voters/

28. https://www.foxnews.com/politics/53k-dead-people-on-floridas-voter-rolls

29. https://pjmedia.com/jchristianadams/2012/5/17/53000-dead-voters-found-in-florida/

30. https://pjmedia.com/jchristianadams/2012/5/17/53000-dead-voters-found-in-florida/

31. https://www.heritage.org/voterfraud/search?combine=lafayette&state=OR&year=&case_type=All&fraud_type=All

32. http://people.reed.edu/~gronkep/docs/Carter%20Baker%20Report-publicrelease.pdf

33. https://www.wausaudailyherald.com/story/news/2018/11/19/wausau-voter-fraud-man-sent-absentee-ballots-dead-mother/2055237002/

34. https://www.nbcnewyork.com/news/local/Dead-Voter-List-Long-Island-Nassau-County-Newsday-230030371.html

Chapter 4

1. https://www.pewtrusts.org/~/media/legacy/uploadedfiles/pcs_assets/2012/pewupgradingvoterregistrationpdf.pdf

2. https://www.justice.gov/crt/title-42-public-health-and-welfare-chapter-20-elective-franchise-subchapter-i-h-national-voter#anchor_1973gg

3. https://ballotpedia.org/Voter_caging_and_purging

4. https://www.cbsnews.com/news/analysis-by-voter-group-finds-dead-people-likely-registered-in-indiana/

5. https://www.theindychannel.com/news/politics/state-police-superintendent-confirms-voter-registration-fraud

6. https://thehill.com/blogs/ballot-box/329659-indiana-purges-nearly-half-a-million-from-voter-rolls

7. https://thehill.com/blogs/ballot-box/329659-indiana-purges-nearly-half-a-million-from-voter-rolls

8. https://www.foxnews.com/politics/thousands-of-dead-people-likely-on-indiana-voter-rolls-analysts-say

9. https://legiscan.com/IN/text/SB0442/id/1580233

10. http://www.projectvote.org/blog/indiana-bill-erroneously-purge-legitimate-voters/

11. https://www.brennancenter.org/legal-work/IndianaNAACP-and-IndianaLWV-v-Lawson

12. https://www.motherjones.com/politics/2018/06/supreme-court-deals-a-blow-to-voting-rights-and-invites-more-states-to-purge-their-rolls/

13. https://www.npr.org/2018/06/11/618870982/supreme-court-upholds-controversial-ohio-voter-purge-law

14. https://www.bizpacreview.com/2018/08/10/lots-of-folks-over-100-years-old-reportedly-on-ohio-voter-rolls-in-hotly-contested-district-662613

15. https://townhall.com/tipsheet/guybenson/2014/04/03/oh-my-evidence-of-massive-voter-fraud-in-north-carolina-n1818137

16. https://townhall.com/tipsheet/guybenson/2014/04/03/oh-my-evidence-of-massive-voter-fraud-in-north-carolina-n1818137

17. https://en.wikipedia.org/wiki/2008_United_States_presidential_election_in_North_Carolina

18. https://www.nccivitas.org/civitas-review/576534-voters-gone-great-north-carolina-voter-purge-2019/

19. https://www.chron.com/news/houston-texas/houston/article/In-wake-of-voter-purge-Andrade-resigns-as-Texas-4055333.php

20. https://www.statesman.com/article/20121004/NEWS/310049617
21. ibid
22. https://www.npr.org/2012/09/16/161145248/many-texans-bereaved-over-dead-voter-purge
23. ibid
24. https://www.judicialwatch.org/document-archive/tag/nvra-violation-letters/
25. https://www.judicialwatch.org/press-room/press-releases/judicial-watch-warns-11-states-clean-voter-registration-lists-face-federal-lawsuit/
26. https://www.judicialwatch.org/blog/2018/10/maryland-implies-judicial-watch-has-ties-to-russian-agents-in-shameful-effort-to-hide-voter-rolls-mess/
27. https://www.judicialwatch.org/press-room/press-releases/judicial-watch-victory-court-ordered-consent-decree-requires-kentucky-to-clean-up-election-rolls/
28. https://www.bizpacreview.com/2019/01/04/judicial-watch-wins-suit-california-forced-to-remove-up-to-1-5-million-inactive-voters-and-clean-up-its-rolls-709972
29. https://www.justice.gov/crt/about-national-voter-registration-act
30. https://www.pewtrusts.org/~/media/legacy/uploaded files/pcs_assets/2012/pewupgradingvoterregistrationpdf.pdf
31. http://www.maciverinstitute.com/2018/06/almost-4000-cases-of-voter-fraud-recorded-by-wisconsin-officials-after-2016-election/
32. https://rightwisconsin.com/2018/06/18/almost-4000-cases-of-likely-voter-fraud-recorded-by-wisconsin-officials-after-2016-election
33. https://www.azcentral.com/story/news/politics/legislature/2019/03/27/arizona-would-purge-voters-early-ballot-list-under-bill/3273394002/
34. https://www.brennancenter.org/publication/purges-growing-threat-right-vote#INTRODUCTION
35. http://maristpoll.marist.edu/wp-content/uploads/2018/09/NPR_Marist-Poll_National-

Nature-of-the-Sample-and-Tables_September-
2018_1809111654.pdf#page=3
36. https://www.brennancenter.org/publication/purges-
growing-threat-right-vote#INTRODUCTION

CHAPTER 5

1. https://www.theepochtimes.com/ballot-harvesting-
helped-flip-seven-california-house-races-after-election-
day_2730138.html
2. https://www.washingtonpost.com/politics/2018/11/2
9/paul-ryan-isnt-saying-there-was-voter-fraud-
california/?utm_term=.beef90eb8579
3. https://www.theepochtimes.com/ballot-harvesting-
helped-flip-seven-california-house-races-after-election-
day_2730138.html
4. https://www.latimes.com/politics/la-me-pol-mimi-
walters-young-kim-201891112-story.html
5. https://ballotpedia.org/Mimi_Walters
6. https://myemail.constantcontact.com/You-Don-t-
Need--Voter-Fraud----When-a-14-point-lead-Disappears---
Shawn-Steel---Washington-
Times.html?soid=1117424089885&aid=UlPJYp3KOYQ
7. https://washingtonbabylon.com/ballot-harvesting-
something-is-rotten-in-california-and-heading-your-way-
soon-2/
8. https://www.wsj.com/articles/harvesting-democratic-
votes-11547856541
9. https://www.wsj.com/articles/californias-vote-
harvesting-pro-and-con-11548612867
10. https://www.wsj.com/articles/harvesting-democratic-
votes-11547856541?mod=article_inline
11. https://www.latimes.com/opinion/editorials/la-ed-
ballot-harvesting-20181207-story.html
12. https://www.phoenixnewtimes.com/news/phoenix-
cops-bash-muslims-immigrants-and-black-people-online-
11306928
13. https://www.nytimes.com/2016/11/06/us/politics/ari
zona-supreme-court-absentee-ballots.html

14. https://www.realclearpolitics.com/articles/2019/03/1
1/ballot_harvesting_divide_persists_amid_elections_debate
.html

15. https://www.cnbc.com/2019/02/18/north-carolina-
9th-district-house-election-saw-ballot-harvesting-
official.html

16. https://fox2now.com/2019/02/18/worker-details-
alleged-ballot-fraud-in-north-carolina-election-board-
hearing/

17. https://www.robesonian.com/opinion/119407/ballot-
harvesting-vs-the-gop

18. https://www.charlotteobserver.com/news/politics-
government/article226864674.html

19. https://thehill.com/homenews/campaign/431023-
north-carolina-elections-board-calls-new-election-in-
contested-house-race

20. https://twitter.com/McCreadyForNC/status/1098697
108595593216?ref_src=twsrc%5Etfw%7Ctwcamp%5Etwe
etem-
bed%7Ctwterm%5E1098697108595593216&ref_url=https
%3A%2F%2Fthehill.com%2Fhomenews%2Fcampaign%2
F431023-north-carolina-elections-board-calls-new-election-
in-contested-house-race

21. https://moritzlaw.osu.edu/election-
law/article/?article=13451

22. https://www.realclearpolitics.com/articles/2019/03/1
1/ballot_harvesting_divide_persists_amid_elections_debate
.html

23. https://www.apnews.com/211109ea75094be396ca9a2
29f169060

24. https://www.realclearpolitics.com/articles/2019/03/0
6/on_ballot_harvesting_gop_may_have_to_push_back.ht
ml

25. https://thefederalist.com/2018/12/14/ballot-
harvesting-became-new-way-steal-election/

26. https://www.washingtonpost.com/politics/we-got-our-
clocks-cleaned-gop-quietly-works-to-expand-ballot-
harvesting-in-california-while-criticizing-democrats-for-the-

practice/2019/03/13/a432d902-41b7-11e9-922c-64d6b7840b82_story.html?noredirect=on&utm_term=.973
23b14c852

27. https://www.realclearinvestigations.com/articles/2018
/12/12/ballot_fraud_american-
style_and_its_bitter_harvests.html#!

28. https://www.palmbeachpost.com/news/opinion/edito
rial-use-voter-fraud-report-fix-absentee-ballot-
system/vWwmNhIZEVMSRvCpWaXSgL/

29. http://www.tampabay.com/news/politics/national/in-
madison-county-floridas-longest-absentee-voter-fraud-
case/1259977

30. http://www.fdle.state.fl.us/News/2011/November/M
adison-County-officials-arrested-for-voter-fraud

31. https://dailycaller.com/2011/11/24/12-charged-with-
voter-fraud-in-georgia-election/

32. https://dailycaller.com/2011/07/29/mississippi-
naacp-leader-sent-to-prison-for-10-counts-of-voter-fraud/

33. https://www.reuters.com/article/us-naacp-
voters/naacp-head-likens-voter-id-measures-to-jim-crow-
idUSTRE76O6NP20110725

34. https://www.realclearinvestigations.com/articles/2018
/12/12/ballot_fraud_american-
style_and_its_bitter_harvests.html#!

35. https://www.questia.com/newspaper/1P2-
40003270/judge-orders-new-election-for-hubbard-franks-
state

36. https://twitter.com/Barnes_Law/status/10690522402
56819200?ref_src=twsrc%5Etfw%7Ctwcamp%5Etweetem
bed%7Ctwterm%5E1069052240256819200&ref_url=https
%3A%2F%2Fwww.americanthinker.com%2Fblog%2F201
8%2F12%2Fthe_stomachturning_ballotharvesting_that_en
abled_democrats_to_walk_off_with_california.html

37. https://www.thegatewaypundit.com/2014/10/caught-
on-tape-dem-operative-stuffs-ballot-box-in-arizona-video/

38. http://vote.caltech.edu/sites/default/files/Voting%20
Technology%20Report_1_14_2013.pdf

39. https://dfw.cbslocal.com/2018/10/25/documents-vote-harvesting-scheme-tarrant-county/

40. https://www.thegatewaypundit.com/2018/12/ballot-harvesting-added-over-250000-votes-in-orange-county-flipping-four-seats-blue/

41. https://dfw.cbslocal.com/2018/10/12/women-accused-paid-voter-fraud-ring/

42. https://www.dallasnews.com/news/texas-legislature/2017/05/10/texas-lawmakers-racing-clock-pass-bill-aimed-curbing-mail-vote-fraud

43. https://www.expressnews.com/news/local/politics/article/Webb-County-mail-in-ballot-fraud-allegations-may-12865196.php

44. https://www.sos.texas.gov/elections/voter/reqabbm.shtml

45. https://nebraska.tv/news/local/several-nebraska-counties-planning-switch-to-all-mail-elections

46. http://www.ncsl.org/research/elections-and-campaigns/all-mail-elections.aspx

47. https://www.electiondefense.org/vote-by-mail

48. https://www.sacbee.com/news/politics-government/capitol-alert/article220581720.html

49. https://townhall.com/columnists/lawrencemeyers/2016/10/06/massive-voter-fraud-sweep-under-way-by-texas-ag-n2228904

Chapter 6

1. https://www.englishforums.com/English/LimitTheSpectrum/blknxj/post.htm

2. https://www.mackinac.org/OvertonWindow

3. https://www.brookings.edu/blog/fixgov/2017/06/21/voter-suppression-and-election-integrity-commission/

4. https://www.politico.com/story/2012/08/why-voter-id-laws-are-like-a-poll-tax-079416

5. https://www.britannica.com/topic/Fifteenth-Amendment

6. https://www.newsmax.com/Politics/eric-holder-attorney-general-voter-suppression-trump/2017/07/25/id/803635/

7. https://observer.com/2017/04/eric-holder-voter-suppression-trump-republicans/

8. https://www.rawstory.com/2019/04/eric-holder-progressives-will-beat-hell-conservatives-fight-fair-elections/

9. https://www.washingtonpost.com/politics/courts_law/getting-a-photo-id-so-you-can-vote-is-easy-unless-youre-poor-black-latino-or-elderly/2016/05/23/8d5474ec-20f0-11e6-8690-f14ca9de2972_story.html?utm_term=.f03258543c68

10. https://slate.com/news-and-politics/2012/08/voter-id-laws-why-do-minorities-lack-id-to-show-at-the-polls.html

11. https://www.youtube.com/watch?v=yW2LpFkVfYk&t=1s

12. https://www.washingtonexaminer.com/24-things-that-require-a-photo-id

13. https://www.youtube.com/watch?v=jUDTcxIqqM0

14. https://www.youtube.com/watch?v=iGcfRbtgVak&feature=youtu.be&t=1141

15. https://www.amazon.com/dp/B017GH546O/ref=dp-kindle-redirect?_encoding=UTF8&btkr=1

16. https://www.ajc.com/news/despite-voter-law-minority-turnout-georgia/3wOfD2SkXmTgRwbySd2ZiK/

17. https://www.povertyactionlab.org/evaluation/effects-voter-id-notification-voter-turnout-united-states

18. https://www.dailysignal.com/2019/02/26/new-study-confirms-voter-id-laws-dont-hurt-election-turnout/

19. https://www.eac.gov/assets/1/6/Exhibit%20M.PDF

20. https://www.heritage.org/election-integrity/commentary/no-hillary-voter-id-laws-dont-suppress-turnout

21. https://www.nationalreview.com/2015/07/voter-id-other-countries-require/

22. https://www.ifes.org/what-we-do

23. https://foreignpolicy.com/2012/11/06/foreign-election-officials-amazed-by-trust-based-u-s-voting-system-2/

24. https://foreignpolicy.com/2012/11/06/foreign-election-officials-amazed-by-trust-based-u-s-voting-system-2/

25. https://www.brennancenter.org/sites/default/files/legacy/publications/Appendix.Mexico.pdf

26. https://epic.org/privacy/voting/crawford/

27. https://www.in.gov/sos/elections/2401.htm

28. https://www.in.gov/sos/elections/2624.htm

29. https://epic.org/privacy/voting/crawford/

30. https://epic.org/privacy/voting/crawford/

31. http://www.ncsl.org/research/elections-and-campaigns/supreme-court-upholds-indiana-photo-id-law.aspx

32. https://www.washingtonpost.com/blogs/blogpost/post/voter-id-proponents-point-to-laws-in-other-countries/2012/07/12/gJQAVlGCfW_blog.html?utm_term=.ee195eb5c80a

33. https://www.nytimes.com/2008/04/29/washington/28cnd-scotus.html

34. https://www.nytimes.com/2008/04/29/washington/28cnd-scotus.html

35. https://thinkprogress.org/north-carolina-voter-law-dead-6dc027569681/

36. https://www.thedailybeast.com/north-carolina-gop-brags-racist-voter-suppression-is-workingand-theyre-right

37. https://www.theguardian.com/world/2013/aug/13/north-carolina-voter-id-law

38. https://www.americanthinker.com/blog/2017/12/how_liberal_is_your_federal_circuit_court.html

39. https://www.washingtonpost.com/politics/courts_law/supreme-court-wont-review-decision-that-found-nc-voting-law-discriminates-against-african-americans/2017/05/15/59425b1c-2368-11e7-a1b3-

faff0034e2de_story.html?noredirect=on&utm_term=.8e0a 32f5e8ac

40. https://www.dailysignal.com/2016/09/04/how-liberal-judges-took-control-of-70-percent-of-us-appeals-courts/

41. https://www.heritage.org/election-integrity/commentary/voter-id-and-the-real-threat-democracy

42. https://www.npr.org/sections/thetwo-way/2017/05/15/528457693/supreme-court-declines-republican-bid-to-revive-north-carolina-voter-id-law

43. http://www.people-press.org/2012/10/11/broad-support-for-photo-id-voting-requirements/

44. https://news.gallup.com/poll/194741/four-five-americans-support-voter-laws-early-voting.aspx

45. https://www.weeklystandard.com/the-majority-of-minorities-support-voter-id-laws/article/2003934

46. https://www.qu.edu/news-and-events/quinnipiac-university-poll/2016-presidential-swing-state-polls/release-detail?ReleaseID=2345

47. http://www.elon.edu/docs/e-web/elonpoll/030413_ElonPoll_voterID.pdf

48. https://www.desmoinesregister.com/story/news/politics/iowa-poll/2017/02/19/iowa-poll-majority-support-mandatory-voter-id/97889850/

49. https://stories.avvo.com/rights/8-disturbing-examples-voter-suppression-in-america.html

50. https://abcnews.go.com/Blotter/Vote2008/story?id=5963751&page=1

51. https://www.nytimes.com/1993/11/11/nyregion/florio-s-defeat-revives-memories-of-gop-activities-in-1981.html

52. https://www.brennancenter.org/legal-work/dnc-v-rnc-consent-decree

53. https://www.facebook.com/princewilliamcountyNAACP/posts/554853518187562

54. https://www.foxnews.com/politics/new-black-panther-leader-defends-group-in-voter-intimidation-case

55. https://www.foxnews.com/politics/new-black-panther-leader-defends-group-in-voter-intimidation-case

56. https://www.thegatewaypundit.com/2010/07/we-will-not-be-silenced-democrats-produce-documentary-alleging-rampant-vote-fraud-by-team-obama/

57. https://www.nytimes.com/2008/10/09/us/politics/09voting.html

58. https://www.denverpost.com/2008/10/09/colorado-disputes-voter-purge/

59. ibid

60. https://news.gallup.com/poll/196976/update-americans-confidence-voting-election.aspx

CHAPTER 7

1. https://www.washingtonpost.com/news/post-politics/wp/2017/05/11/white-house-to-launch-a-commission-to-study-voter-fraud-and-suppression/?utm_term=.322e1ae1fd5a

2. https://epic.org/privacy/litigation/voter/epic-v-commission/

3. https://www.washingtonpost.com/blogs/wonkblog/files/2017/06/PEIC-Letter-to-Connecticut-1.pdf

4. https://www.nytimes.com/2018/01/03/us/politics/trump-voter-fraud-commission.html

5. https://www.zerohedge.com/news/2017-07-01/what-are-they-trying-hide-trump-asks-after-29-states-refuse-give-data-voter-fraud-pa

6. https://www.nytimes.com/2018/01/03/us/politics/trump-voter-fraud-commission.html

7. https://www.naacpldf.org/files/about-us/EIC%20Complaint.pdf

8. http://www.electionlawcenter.com/uncategorized/statement-on-presidential-advisory-commission-on-election-integrity/

9. https://www.naacpldf.org/files/about-us/EIC%20Complaint.pdf

10. https://www.brookings.edu/blog/fixgov/2017/06/21/voter-suppression-and-election-integrity-commission/

11. https://www.brookings.edu/blog/fixgov/2017/06/21/
voter-suppression-and-election-integrity-commission/
12. https://obamawhitehouse.archives.gov/the-press-
office/2013/03/28/executive-order-establishment-
presidential-commission-election-administr

CHAPTER 8

1. https://www.projectveritas.com/2019/06/24/insider-
blows-whistle-exec-reveals-google-plan-to-prevent-trump-
situation-in-2020-on-hidden-cam/
2. https://twitter.com/JamesOKeefeIII/status/11432569
92431136768?ref_src=twsrc%5Etfw%7Ctwcamp%5Etwee
tem-
bed%7Ctwterm%5E1143256992431136768&ref_url=https
%3A%2F%2Fboundingintocomics.com%2F2019%2F06%
2F25%2Fnew-google-leak-appears-to-contradict-google-
executive-jen-gennais-response-to-project-veritas-video%2F
3. https://www.projectveritas.com/wp-
content/uploads/2019/06/Senator-Cruz-Veritas-Google-
Report.pdf
4. https://medium.com/@gennai.jen/this-is-not-how-i-
expected-monday-to-go-e92771c7aa82
5. https://www.projectveritas.com/2019/06/25/breaking
-new-google-document-leaked-describing-shapiro-prager-
as-nazis-using-the-dogwhistles/
6. http://fm.cnbc.com/applications/cnbc.com/resources
/styles/skin/special-reports/pdfs/russian-active-
measures.pdf
7. https://www.politico.com/magazine/story/2015/08/h
ow-google-could-rig-the-2016-election-121548
8. https://www.pnas.org/content/pnas/early/2015/08/0
3/1419828112.full.pdf
9. https://www.scribd.com/document/377329039/Epstei
n-Mohr-Martinez-2018-Wpa-The-Search-Suggestion-
Effect-sse-wp-17-
03?secret_password=qZ8JSbCYbcGWGNdRiFIo
10. https://www.newsweek.com/republicans-furious-
google-over-gop-nazi-link-956770

11. https://www.usatoday.com/story/opinion/2018/09/1
0/trump-google-youtube-search-results-biased-against-
republicans-conservatives-column/1248099002/
12. https://wikileaks.org/podesta-emails/emailid/37262
13. https://www.facebook.com/SourceFedNews/videos/1
199514293432055/
14. https://thefederalist.com/2016/06/10/is-google-
manipulating-search-results-to-help-hillary-clinton/
15. https://money.cnn.com/2016/06/10/technology/hilla
ry-clinton-google-search-results/index.html
16. https://www.politico.com/magazine/story/2015/08/h
ow-google-could-rig-the-2016-election-121548
17. https://www.usnews.com/opinion/articles/2016-06-
22/google-is-the-worlds-biggest-censor-and-its-power-must-
be-regulated
18. https://www.usnews.com/opinion/articles/2016-06-
22/google-is-the-worlds-biggest-censor-and-its-power-must-
be-regulated
19. https://spreadprivacy.com/google-filter-bubble-study/
20. https://www.politico.com/magazine/story/2015/08/h
ow-google-could-rig-the-2016-election-121548
21. https://spreadprivacy.com/google-filter-bubble-study/
22. https://www.breitbart.com/tech/2019/03/07/leaked-
audio-google-discusses-steering-the-conservative-
movement/
23. https://www.realclearpolitics.com/video/2018/09/11
/tucker_carlson_did_google_meddle_in_2016_election_mo
re_than_russia.html
24. https://www.breitbart.com/tech/2018/09/12/leaked-
video-google-leaderships-dismayed-reaction-to-trump-
election/
25. https://medium.com/@mikewacker/googles-manual-
interventions-in-search-results-a3b0cfd3e26c
26. https://medium.com/@mikewacker/googles-manual-
interventions-in-search-results-a3b0cfd3e26c
27. https://dailycaller.com/2019/04/09/google-news-
blacklist-search-manipulation/

28. https://www.breitbart.com/tech/2019/01/16/google-youtube-search-blacklist-smoking-gun/

29. https://twitter.com/realDonaldTrump/status/103445 6273306243076

30. https://www.wsj.com/articles/google-workers-discussed-tweaking-search-function-to-counter-travel-ban-1537488472

CHAPTER 9

1. https://www.history.com/topics/black-history/fifteenth-amendment

2. https://www.history.com/topics/womens-history/19th-amendment-1

3. https://en.wikipedia.org/wiki/Indian_Citizenship_Act

4. https://en.wikipedia.org/wiki/Timeline_of_voting_rig hts_in_the_United_States

5. https://www.fairvote.org/voter_turnout#voter_turnout _101

6. https://www8.nationalacademies.org/onpinews/newsit em.aspx?RecordID=25120

7. https://www.nap.edu/catalog/25120/securing-the-vote-protecting-american-democracy

8. https://www.sandiegouniontribune.com/news/us-politics/la-na-pol-voting-by-phone-20190516-story.html

9. https://www8.nationalacademies.org/onpinews/newsit em.aspx?RecordID=25120

10. https://www.wired.com/2014/01/tech-time-warp-ibm-ramac/

11. https://richtopia.com/emerging-technologies/11-disruptive-technology-examples

12. https://www.latimes.com/politics/la-na-pol-voting-by-phone-20190516-story.html

13. https://www.verifiedvoting.org/resources/internet-voting/

14. https://www.latimes.com/politics/la-na-pol-voting-by-phone-20190516-story.html

15. https://portswigger.net/daily-swig/smartphone-voting-brings-new-security-concerns

16. https://www.venafi.com/blog/venafi-study-election-infrastructure-risk

17. https://www.wired.com/story/smartphone-voting-is-happening-west-virginia/

18. ibid

19. https://www.latimes.com/politics/la-na-pol-voting-by-phone-20190516-story.html

20. https://people.eng.unimelb.edu.au/vjteague/HowNot ToProveElectionOutcome.pdf

21. https://www.cyberscoop.com/swiss-voting-system-flaw-encryption/

22. https://www.verifiedvoting.org/resources/voting-equipment/

23. https://ballotpedia.org/Voting_methods_and_equipme nt_by_state#cite_note-verify-1

24. Ibid

25. https://www.cbsnews.com/news/rigged-presidential-elections-hackers-demonstrate-voting-threat-old-machines/

26. https://www.newsweek.com/election-hacking-voting-machines-software-1028948

27. https://www.businessinsider.com/election-systems-and-software-admits-shipping-vote-systems-with-key-flaw-2018-7/

28. https://twitter.com/RonWyden?ref_src=twsrc%5Etfw %7Ctwcamp%5Etweetembed%7Ctwterm%5E101927536 2344296451%7Ctwgr%5E393039363b636f6e74726f6c&re f_url=https%3A%2F%2Fwww.newsweek.com%2Felection -hacking-voting-machines-software-1028948

29. https://fortune.com/2017/07/28/russia-election-hacking-def-con/

30. https://www.newyorker.com/news/dispatch/election-hacking-lessons-from-the-2018-def-con-hackers-conference

31. https://www.chron.com/news/politics/texas/article/V oting-machine-errors-changed-some-Texans-13339298.php

32. https://www.theverge.com/2018/10/30/18037872/te xas-voting-machine-hart-eslate-voting-ballot-switch-problems

33. https://www.huffpost.com/entry/ky-election-officials-arr_b_177468

34. https://www.greensboro.com/news/voting-machine-again-displays-wrong-choice/article_4b6f41e4-616e-11e4-aa89-0017a43b2370.html#.VFexxsO-0mo.twitter

35. https://www.foxnews.com/politics/calibration-error-changes-gop-votes-to-dem-in-illinois-county

36. https://townhall.com/tipsheet/katiepavlich/2014/10/28/voting-machine-in-maryland-changes-votes-for-republicans-to-votes-for-democrats-n1910991

37. https://www.thestate.com/news/state/south-carolina/article221190430.html

38. https://pittsburgh.cbslocal.com/2016/11/08/some-problems-reported-as-voters-head-to-polls/

39. https://techcrunch.com/2019/03/27/senators-security-voting-machines/

40. https://www.klobuchar.senate.gov/public/index.cfm/2019/4/klobuchar-urges-department-of-homeland-security-and-fbi-to-establish-election-security-task-force

41. https://www.cyberscoop.com/secure-elections-act-reintroduced/

42. http://www.startribune.com/klobuchar-s-secure-elections-act-stalls/492047171/

43. https://www.ajc.com/news/state--regional-govt--politics/georgia-lawmakers-prepare-for-fight-over-switch-paper-ballots/55mAQSHQPFSqniXARCbxzN/

CHAPTER 11

1. https://www.wnd.com/2016/12/trumps-landslide-2623-to-489-among-u-s-counties/

2. https://www.dailymail.co.uk/news/article-4055182/Final-tally-shows-Trump-lost-popular-vote-2-8-million-BEAT-Clinton-3-million-votes-outside-California-New-York.html

3. https://www.dailymail.co.uk/news/article-4055182/Final-tally-shows-Trump-lost-popular-vote-2-8-

million-BEAT-Clinton-3-million-votes-outside-California-New-York.html

4. https://www.verifiedvoting.org/voting-system-principles/

5. https://www.youtube.com/watch?v=O8ISoeO1hjw&feature=emb_logo

6. https://ericstates.org/

About the Author

ADRIAN NORMAN is an author, columnist and political commentator. His passion for helping people better navigate toxic political and news environments is second only to his appreciation for maple-cured bacon. Norman is also a member of the black leadership network Project 21, a division of the National Center for Public Policy Research, which addresses regulatory policy, fiscal policy, national defense and environmental policy, among other issues.

Made in the USA
San Bernardino, CA
01 July 2020

74546618R00166